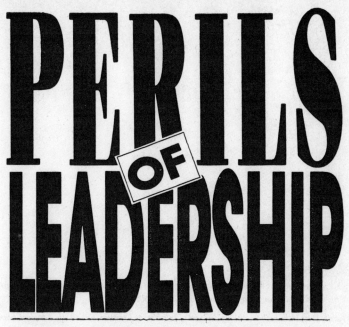

# PERILS OF LEADERSHIP

## Overcoming Personal Battles

# KENNETH PRIOR

With Study Questions
for Individuals or Groups

INTERVARSITY PRESS
DOWNERS GROVE, ILLINOIS 60515

InterVarsity Press is the book-publishing division of InterVarsity Christian Fellowship, a student movement active on campus at hundreds of universities, colleges and schools of nursing. For information about local and regional activities, write Public Relations Dept., InterVarsity Christian Fellowship, 6400 Schroeder Rd., P.O. Box 7895, Madison, WI 53707-7895.

Distributed in Canada through InterVarsity Press, 860 Denison St., Unit 3, Markham, Ontario L3R 4H1, Canada.

All Scripture quotations, unless otherwise indicated, are from the Holy Bible, New International Version. Copyright © 1973, 1978, International Bible Society. Used by permission of Zondervan Bible Publishers.

Cover background: Roberta Polfus

ISBN 0-8308-1299-7

Printed in the United States of America ∞

**Library of Congress Cataloging-in-Publication Data**

Prior, Kenneth Francis William.
    Perils of leadership/Kenneth Prior.
        p.    cm.
    Includes bibliographical references.
    ISBN 0-8308-1299-7
    1. Christian leadership.    2. Christian leadership—Biblical
teaching.    I. Title.
    BV652.1.P72    1990
    253'.2—dc20                                                90-4055
                                                                    CIP

16    15    14    13    12    11    10    9    8    7    6    5    4    3    2    1
99    98    97    96    95    94    93    92    91    90

# Introduction

Charles Spurgeon, a nineteenth-century Baptist preacher, asked in one of his lectures: "As to mental maladies, is any man altogether sane? Are we not all a little off-balance?" He was accounting for what he called (in the title of this particular lecture) "The Minister's fainting fits." He was recognizing that Christian leaders are human and can be afflicted by emotional difficulties, such as depression, as much as anyone else. According to Spurgeon, "The strong are not always vigorous, the wise not always ready, the brave not always courageous, and the joyous not always happy." Indeed, the pressures of ministry, the deep concerns which accompany it and the expectations which others have, may render leaders more subject to such problems than others.

Much help is available from secular sources such as counseling and management studies, and we would be foolish to ignore it and fail to use the insights into our problems which it provides. Such help, however, does have limitations for Christian leaders. How can we expect to find a complete answer to our needs if God and the work of the Holy Spirit are left out? Indeed, Christians will want to test ideas from psychology and from other secular sources in the light of the teaching of Scripture.

When we turn to Scripture, and especially to a study of biblical leaders, we are not disappointed. None of them were superhuman, and yet God used them. Not only did they share our sinful nature, but we find among them examples of all of the fleshly weaknesses typical of fallen persons today—depression, hypersensitivity, inadequacy, anxiety and immaturity. Like us, they experienced family problems, opposition from the world and criticism from church members as cruel as anything found today. Because they were human, they felt these pressures as acutely as any of us would. Elijah, one of the outstanding leaders of the Old Testament, was described by James as "a man of like nature with ourselves" (Jas 5:17). Paul too was aware that God had committed the gospel to very ordinary men when he wrote, "we have this treasure in jars of clay" (2 Cor 4:7).

This is not a book about Bible characters. Anyone looking for a complete exposition of the lives of the examples I have chosen will be disappointed. Nor am I writing simply about how these men exercised their leadership. Rather, I am looking at their personal problems and how God either overcame them or enabled these men to live with them and even to use them for his glory.

I am not aware that much has been written on this subject from a biblical standpoint in recent times, so this book is not a rehash of what others have written. I am, however, indebted to many who have unknowingly contributed to these studies—past colleagues and church members, many who have shown patience with my own failures. In particular I would like to mention the Reverend Dr. Roger Curl. He was my colleague for only three months, but has become a close friend. He is a capable expositor of Scripture and a sociologist as well, which means that his understanding of these matters is both biblically sound and grounded in human reality. His encouragement and advice have proven invaluable.

I have personally gained much from preparing this book and have received yet another reminder of the relevance of Scripture to our real needs. All of the problems which I have been conscious of in myself, and which I have detected in fellow ministers, I have found addressed in Scripture. My main regret is that I did not undertake these studies at the beginning of my ministry. Facing up to our weaknesses is essential for all of us— no matter how successful we think ourselves to be—if we are to avoid the danger Paul warned of: "Lest after preaching to others I myself should be disqualified" ( 1 Cor 9:27 RSV).

# 1

# IMMATURITY

## Joseph

JOSEPH IS THE FIRST LEADER WE ENCOUNTER IN THE OLD TESTA-ment, and it is difficult to imagine a more outstanding example. Brought up as a country boy in an unknown family in the land of Canaan, he rose to become Secretary of State of Egypt, at that time the most powerful and highly civilized nation in the Middle East. In this position he made his mark on Old Testament history, as he was able to establish the people of God in Egypt. The reason for this was later revealed to Jacob when God said to him, "Do not be afraid to go down to Egypt, for I will make you into a great nation there" (Gen 46:3).

Why was Egypt the place for them to become "a great nation"? There seem to have been two main reasons. First, they needed a place to expand. For more than two hundred years

Abraham and his descendants had been wandering as pilgrims. In spite of God's promise to make of Abraham a great nation, few children had yet been born. "After two centuries one tent could contain the whole male population."[1] But in Jacob's time the family began to increase. His twelve sons (which the twelve tribes of Israel descended from) were many more than either Isaac or Abraham had produced. There were signs that growth into a nation, which God had promised, was now beginning to happen. But a critical point was approaching. They would soon be large enough to constitute a challenge to the surrounding tribes, who would hardly take kindly to their conviction that they were God's special choice. At the same time, it would take a few more generations before they were large enough to defend themselves. This critical point had to be passed. God's answer was to take them to Egypt where they could expand unmolested.

There was another advantage to be gained from Egypt. There they could have contact with the most civilized people of that time, an experience which was far removed from the semi-barbarous life they knew in Canaan. Moses (who was ultimately to lead them out of Egypt) was, as Stephen many centuries later pointed out, "instructed in all the wisdom of the Egyptians" (Acts 7:22 RSV). So, when Joseph used his position to bring his family to Egypt, although probably unaware of it, he was pioneering a great movement. Who, then, was this Joseph, who was to occupy such a significant place in history?

## Joseph's Immaturity
Our story begins in Genesis 37 when Joseph was seventeen, and, looking at it simply as a human story (God is not mentioned in that chapter), a most unpromising beginning it is. In verse 3 we are told that he was Jacob's favorite son, and one

of the ways in which Jacob expressed his love was by giving Joseph "a long robe with sleeves." This was a flowing robe worn by an official who did no manual work. If anyone in the family was entitled to wear such a garment, it was Reuben, the eldest, not Joseph. Such treatment can do untold harm, producing a self-centered personality. In Joseph's case it led to severe difficulties in his relationship with his half-brothers. A literal translation of verse 3 could be "he kept making him a long robe with sleeves." As soon as one wore out, he made another. So the irritation to the rest of the family was continuous, and the effect was that "they hated him and could not speak peaceably to him" (v. 4).

There were, of course, reasons that Jacob pampered him. One was that he "was the son of his old age" (v. 3). He had to wait a long time for a child by Rachel, the favorite of his two wives. So when Joseph was born, he was immediately the object of special favor. Then to make matters worse, while Joseph was still a child, his mother died in childbirth and so "into his life is poured all the over-stressed affection his father had felt for Rachel."[2] There may have been reasons, but that does not excuse Jacob. "Can Jacob have forgotten" asks Alexander Whyte, "the sea of trouble into which his father's favoritism, and his mother's indulgence, cast both themselves and their children?"[3]

Genesis 37 gives us three significant incidents. In verse 2 Joseph tells his father what his brothers have been doing. They may well have been doing wrong, and perhaps it was good for Jacob to know, but this kind of behavior was no credit to Joseph. Then there was his dream about the sheaves in which he fantasized about his own destined greatness (vv. 5-8). No doubt all the family had to keep quiet while this wonder-boy was speaking. Then he had another similar dream which was so outrageous that even his father took exception to it (vv. 9-11).

There is an important lesson here. It is possible to be highly gifted, as Joseph undoubtedly was, but lacking in graces. The gifts can even be described as "spiritual" yet the possessor can be very deficient in humility, wisdom and understanding. It is perhaps fitting that Joseph is the first of our examples, because he is typical of the way that many a young leader sets out on his or her life's work. Some of us blush when we recall how we emerged from college convinced that we knew all the answers and that we were God's special gift to the church. We may have begun our ministry with great academic achievements behind us, having read all the right books and become expert at modern methods of communication. Perhaps we had dreams of our future success and fame. But there is more to spiritual leadership than head knowledge and leadership skills. Personal spiritual qualities are called for, and unless we grow out of the kind of immaturity we see in Joseph, those dreams will never be realized in a way that glorifies God.

One area in which difficulties will be experienced is in relationships with those we are trying to lead. The reaction of Joseph's brothers demonstrates this. In Christian leadership we have to cope with people who are sinners like ourselves with their own fleshly weaknesses to be reckoned with. It is all too easy for our own faults to provoke corresponding failings in others and be a cause of stumbling which is patently undesirable in a leader.

This danger is obvious in the case of Joseph in his early days when his attitude simply aroused jealousy in his brothers. Because of his father's treatment of him, they already hated him" (v. 4), and the way Joseph recounted his dreams added to their jealousy (v. 11). This is a perfect example of James's observation that "where you have envy and selfish ambition, there you find disorder and every evil practice" (Jas 3:16). Joseph had the selfish ambition, and his brothers responded with jealousy.

The rest of the story in Genesis 37 is well known to Bible readers. Joseph was sent by his father on an errand to his brothers, who were looking after the sheep. When they saw him approaching in the distance, they began discussing how much they hated him. Their first plan was murder, but this was dropped, and instead they sold him as a slave to traders who were on their way to Egypt. The story is resumed in chapter 39 with Joseph entering his new life as a slave in Egypt.

### The LORD Was with Joseph

It is at this point, after a chapter in which a human situation is described without any mention of the name of God, that the most important factor in Joseph's life is revealed—"The LORD was with Joseph" (Gen 39:2), and this is repeated as a refrain throughout chapter 39. So Joseph is not to be dismissed as a young man with fantastic ego-centered ideas. As the story proceeds, it becomes increasingly clear that there were more than human factors at work. God had his hand on Joseph's life; Joseph's dreams expressed something of the destiny God was planning for him. His father also may have suspected this when Joseph described his dream earlier in the story, because we are told that even though he reprimanded his son, he "kept the saying in mind" (37:11 RSV).

What follows is an example of God's wisdom in using varying circumstances with perfect timing. Joseph's status as a slave could not be further removed from the heights which he was to ascend, but this was God's way of bringing him to Egypt. As a slave he did well, but just as his fortunes were taking a turn for the better he landed in prison, accused of an offense of which he was innocent. This brought him into contact with Pharaoh's butler and baker. When the former was restored to his duties in Pharaoh's court, this seemed to Joseph a golden opportunity for his case to be brought to the attention of the highest authority in the land. But God was concerned with more than Joseph's release. So God used the forgetfulness of the butler to keep Joseph in prison for a further two years and, as often happens, God's delay concealed a greater purpose than Joseph could have imagined. Here was a case of perfect timing. Joseph was still in prison when Pharaoh had the dreams which jogged the butler's memory. Joseph was sent for, and within half an hour or so he was the Secretary of State of Egypt. So by a long and tortuous route, Joseph had now arrived at the position God had intended for him all along.

Similarly, all who have been truly called by God into Christian leadership can look back and trace his hand in the path they have followed. Some of the apparent setbacks which were hard to understand at the time, have proved to be God's way of bringing them to the right place at the right time.

### Training for Leadership

Joseph, however, was not just being maneuvered into position. He had much to learn. Unless he grew out of his immaturity, his fitness for the great responsibilities ahead would be seriously impaired. To begin with, there was the matter of his dreams. They were so characteristic of Joseph that his brothers called him "that dreamer" (Gen 37:19). Here is a lesson for those with gifts of imagination, who first rehearse their future plans in that realm. Rudyard Kipling included this among the ingredients which constitute a mature personality in his well-known poem *If*:

If you can dream—and not make dreams your master;
If you can think—and not make thoughts your aim.

Joseph's visions of grandeur had to be brought down to earth.

He had to realize that small things accomplished matter much more than big things only dreamed of. He had to prove himself as a humble slave and a prisoner, before God entrusted him with greater things. And he did this through God's enabling. When he was a slave, his "master saw that the LORD was with him and that the LORD gave him success in everything he did" (39:3). When he became a prisoner, "the LORD was with him; showed him kindness and granted him favor in the eyes of the prison warden" (39:21).

Jesus stressed the principle that "whoever can be trusted with very little can also be trusted with much" (Lk 16:10). Many of those who have become distinguished church leaders have first proved themselves in a small work. I am reminded of Hudson Taylor, who felt it necessary to prove he could trust God in the comfortable lifestyle in England, before he ventured to trust him as a pioneer missionary in China. A twentieth century example which comes readily to mind is Dr. Martyn Lloyd-Jones, who first proved his ministry in a little-known place in Wales, undertaking a work which was small in comparison with what lay before him at Westminster Chapel in London and beyond. The same principle can be applied in industry when the head of a firm insists that his son first prove himself on the shop floor before sharing in management.

In contrast some of us expect to fulfil our grandiose dreams immediately. I think of newly ordained pastors who treat their congregations to an impressive series of sermons, or deal with some of the time-honored problems in Scripture which have often perplexed more experienced Christians, before they have learned to expound some of the simpler gospel texts.

Joseph also needed to be humbled so that he could handle in a more mature fashion the big ideas his father had given him—which found expression in his dreams. This was even more necessary because they represented God's will for him. But Joseph needed to learn what many a potential leader has to grasp, "that mere youthful confidence and energy, are not the qualities that overcome the world."[4] Peter, having addressed mature leaders and called on the younger church members to submit to their leadership, wrote, "All of you, clothe yourselves with humility toward one another, because 'God opposes the proud, but gives grace to the humble.' Humble yourselves, therefore, under God's mighty hand, that he may lift you up in due time" (1 Pet 5:5-6).

God certainly intended to exalt Joseph, but how was he to make Joseph humble? We don't usually become humble just by being told to be. If we do try, our "humility" is usually unreal and more reminiscent of Uriah Heep than of what is needed in a Christian leader. We usually learn humility by the way we respond to the trials of life. It is the kind of treatment which many potential leaders have to undergo. It was one of the main purposes of the wilderness wanderings for the whole of Israel. Moses told them as those wanderings drew to a close: "Remember how the LORD your God led you all the way in the desert these forty years, to humble you" (Deut 8:2). This humbling process was undoubtedly painful for Joseph.

A leader has to cope with disappointment and failure. This too is a mark of maturity for Kipling:

If you can meet with Triumph and Disaster
And treat those two impostors just the same.

Paul claimed that he could do just that when he wrote from prison: "I know what it is to be in need, and I know what it is to have plenty. I have learned the secret of being content in any and every situation, whether well fed or hungry, whether living in plenty or in want" (Phil 4:12).

After dreaming of greatness, it must have been shattering for

Joseph to find himself a slave in a strange land. But he made the best of the situation and excelled in so doing. His success came to an abrupt end, however, when he was unjustly committed to prison. Again he conducted himself wisely and within the limitations of prison life. He continued to show those very qualities which would be needed when he rose to leadership in Egypt. Again he had to accept a trying situation as he patiently waited two years for the butler to bring his case to the attention of Pharaoh. But all this is what a Christian leader must reckon with. He must persevere in good works in spite of discouragement and never allow himself to become disillusioned. Here is a further mark of maturity which Kipling recognized:

> Or watch the things you gave your life to broken,
> And stoop and build 'em up with worn-out tools.

For any Christian there is encouragement to do this in the promise that "at the proper time we will reap a harvest if we do not give up" (Gal 6:9)—a verse which could well be hung on the wall of many a ministerial study!

A Christian leader must be of sound moral character, not least in the realm of sex. No doubt Paul had this in mind when he insisted that a church leader must be "the husband of but one wife" (1 Tim 3:2). In a world where sexual laxity was commonplace, it was essential for a Christian leader to be above reproach in this area. It is no less essential today for a Christian leader to be stable in relationships with the opposite sex. Here is an area where much dishonor can be brought on the Lord's name; instability in this realm is surely a disqualification for Christian leadership.

Joseph was tested in this sphere and proved himself to be sound in spite of the poor example of some members of his own family. The test to which he was subjected was a severe one. Temptation came to him, as it so often does, when things were beginning to go well. When his master's wife tried to seduce him, it was difficult to avoid her company and it went on day after day. How easy it could have been for Joseph to succumb! There were arguments in favor of so doing. He could be sure of many favors if he gave in to her—perhaps even release from slavery. On the other hand, she might not take kindly to being rebuffed by a slave, as proved to be the case. His response was unequivocal: "How then could I do such a wicked thing and sin against God?" (Gen 39:9).

The temptation was blocked by a standard deeply ingrained in his conscience, so he was shocked at the suggestion. There is no harm in being easily shocked by sin, for it is when we cease to be shocked that we are weaker in the face of temptation. He called the suggested offense by its proper names—not an indiscretion but "wickedness" and "sin." God's word was laid upon his heart that he might not sin against God, as the writer of Psalm 119 also testified (v. 11).

Every test to which Joseph was subjected he came through with flying colors. So when he ultimately appeared before Pharaoh, he was ready for the challenge to be laid before him.

**The Mature Leader**
After a long and tortuous route, Joseph had reached, at the early age of thirty, the highest position to which anyone could rise. To his sudden promotion were added an Egyptian name and an Egyptian bride. At last he was able to use his organizational abilities as he prepared Egypt for the seven years of famine that lay ahead. Here was the greatest test of all—how would this young man, who had dreamed of father, mother and brothers bowing before him, behave now? Would his elevation lead to pride and a fall? Joseph was fighting the same enemy as before—but the missiles being hurled at him were different.

I remember Major Allister Smith recounting the early days of the Salvation Army and the persecution they often suffered—"The world threw bricks at us then. Now they throw bouquets. I sometimes think that the bouquets do us more harm than the bricks ever did."

Let's face it—there can be considerable kudos in Christian leadership. There is a prestige in mounting the pulpit steps, especially for those with large congregations. The spiritual perils of prominence are considerable. It is all too easy for successful Christian leaders to develop an exaggerated view of their own importance. This danger can appear right at the beginning of ministry. One week they are just one of many students listening to lectures. The next week they are the center of attraction as the new minister. They soon feel the preacher's temptation to include in sermon illustrations details which give glory to themselves but add nothing to the truth being proclaimed. James Denney once issued this often quoted warning, "No man can give at once the impression that he himself is clever and that Jesus Christ is mighty to save."

Happily, Joseph was free of any sign of pride or arrogance, for God had refined him through the disciplines of the previous years. Joseph showed mature leadership through loyalty to Pharaoh, as he strengthened Pharaoh's throne. During the famine, Joseph allowed the people to sell their land to Pharaoh in order to buy food. When life returned to normal, all of the land had been nationalized and the former owners were now Pharaoh's tenants. They were allowed to keep four-fifths of their crops and were required to give one-fifth to Pharaoh. Thus, he was faithful to the people as well as to Pharaoh, and they thanked Joseph for saving their lives (Gen 47:13-25).

If a young leader is appointed to serve under an older supervisor, then his or her prime duty is to strengthen the senior's position and to shun any temptation to undermine it. The increasing use of lay leaders is a healthy development in the church, but their newly found authority is to be used to uphold the overall leadership and not to rival it. There are churches today where this especially needs saying.

The way Joseph responded to his brothers when they appeared before him to buy grain is impressive. At first sight his treatment of them may seem somewhat vindictive. A closer study, however, shows that he was trying to discover any change of heart on their part and whether they had repented of their treatment of him thirteen years previously. This he did by a skillful device. He forced them to bring Benjamin with them on their return visit, so that he could see whether they would treat him in the same way as they had treated Joseph. The moving plea of Judah and his offer of himself as a slave so that Benjamin could return home, told Joseph all he wanted to know. The effect was such that he broke down into tears before he revealed his identity to them (44:18—45:3). He then revealed that he had forgiven them and that they could forgive themselves (45:5).

## Joseph's God-centered Outlook
The kind of leader Joseph proved himself to be is a remarkable advance from his beginnings as the pampered son of an indulgent father. Why had Joseph so obviously profited from the hardships and frustrations of his first thirteen years in Egypt? The grim times he had been through could have broken him completely. He might have been filled with resentment and rendered himself quite unfit to be the leader of others. Or he could have been so disillusioned as to make it appear pointless to resist the temptation that came to him with such persistence in Potiphar's house. How was it that he responded so positively

to the severe testing he underwent?

Joseph, in spite of his youth and immaturity, possessed something which is the greatest need of a leader in the work of God—a God-centered outlook. As we should expect, this is where teaching on leadership from secular sources falls short of what is called for in Christian leadership. Joseph's God-centered outlook was expressed in many ways. First, there was his motivation—a desire for God's glory, which contributed to the victorious way in which he coped with his hardships, temptations and frustrations as a slave and a prisoner. This desire for God's glory marked him out as a man of God revealing his potentiality as a great spiritual leader. Evidence of this motivation emerged soon after his arrival in Egypt. His successful time as a slave revealed his natural ability, but he determined that God should receive the glory so that "his master saw that the LORD was with him and that the LORD gave him success in everything he did" (39:3). When tempted, he demonstrated that he knew that sin is "against God," and it was this that mattered most of all.

His overriding concern to please God did not mean that he was unconcerned for others. Joseph showed his fitness to be a leader by the way he was interested in the needs of others, even while in prison. As a result, he was given charge over the other prisoners. His concern for their well-being encouraged the butler and baker to confide to him the dreams which were worrying them. But before helping them with their dreams, he assured them that "interpretations belong to God" (40:8). And when at last he faced his great opportunity with Pharaoh, he disassociated himself from the magic Pharaoh was accustomed to look for by pointing out, "I cannot do it, but God will give Pharaoh the answer he desires" (41:16).

When Joseph then unfolded to Pharaoh the significance of his dream, he placed a strong emphasis on the sovereignty of

God in both giving Pharoah his dream and bringing about the events to which it pointed. As Joseph spelled out the qualifications needed to supervise the preparations for facing the coming crisis, it became clear to Pharaoh the situation demanded someone with more than natural gifts. "Can we find anyone like this man," he asked, "one in whom is the Spirit of God?" (41:38). Thirteen years of testing had proven Joseph was that man.

Further expressions of his God-centeredness came to the fore after he attained his exalted position as Secretary of State for Egypt. What now emerged was a deep conviction that his triumph over the trials he had endured was ultimately due, not to any virtue in himself, but to the sovereign grace of God. As a result, he was able to put it all behind him as he devoted himself to the tasks ahead. This was eloquently expressed in the naming of the sons who were born to him in Egypt: "Joseph named his first-born Manasseh, and said, 'It is because God has made me forget all my trouble and all my father's household.' The second son he named Ephraim and said, 'It is because God has made me fruitful in the land of my suffering' " (41:51-52).

He could have constantly dwelt on the difficult times he had been through (like the person who is always talking about their difficult operation). Deep-seated memories of the early years, when he was pampered by his indulgent father on the one side and hated by his envious brothers on the other, could have made him a candidate for the psychiatrist's couch. But God had healed his memories. That he had lived a useful life during those difficult years of slavery and imprisonment he also attributed to the sovereignty of God. There is no suggestion that he took any credit to himself for the position he had attained or his fitness for it. As another leader many centuries later was to affirm, "By the grace of God I am what I am" (1 Cor 15:10).

Joseph's deep conviction about the sovereignty of God was what helped him to forgive his brothers. Behind their evil deed of selling him into slavery in Egypt, he discovered the hand of God. Here was how he explained it to them: "And now, do not be distressed and do not be angry with yourselves for selling me here, because it was to save lives that God sent me ahead of you." (45:5)

They were still not convinced that Joseph had really forgiven them, because after the death of their father, they wondered whether Joseph would then take action against them. But, as they discovered, their fears were unwarranted. Joseph was upset that they still doubted his forgiveness and were prepared to recount a fictitious message from their father to ensure his favor. So while still recognizing their evil intentions of many years ago, he assured them again of the sovereignty of God over their actions: "You intended to harm me, but God intended it for good, to accomplish what is now being done, the saving of many lives" (50:20).

The most outstanding example in history of the way that God uses even the sins of humanity to work his sovereign will is, of course, the crucifixion of our Lord. That was surely the most wicked deed which sinful humanity ever contrived. Yet, as Peter affirmed on the Day of Pentecost, "This man was handed over to you by God's set purpose and foreknowledge" (Acts 2:23). We must not fail to see the relevance of this God-centered emphasis for these days when so much advice on leadership and other contemporary issues expresses the natural self-centeredness in the thinking of fallen humanity.

Joseph, given the kind of upbringing he had received and the trials he had undergone, could have turned away from God. He could have fallen into self-centered introspection, constantly nurturing a sense of hurt and bitterness against those who had ill-treated him. God, however, had caused him to forget it all—"all my hardship and all my father's house" (41:51 RSV). The healing of those memories had taken place under a realization of the sovereignty of God, enabling Joseph to throw himself wholeheartedly into all that lay before him.

## Questions for Individuals or Groups

1. What difficulties did being his father's favorite son create for Joseph? (pp. 12-13)

2. What were the early signs that Joseph was self-centered? (pp. 13-14)

3. When have you seen people use their spiritual gifts ineffectively because of immaturity? (p. 14)

4. How did Joseph's pride lead to his being sold into slavery? (pp. 14-15).

5. How did the apparent setbacks in Joseph's life lead to his ministry opportunities? (p. 16) How have (what you thought were) setbacks been opportunities for growth for your ministry?

6. How did Joseph's years in slavery improve his personality? (pp. 18-19)

7. While serving under Pharaoh, Joseph could have become prideful. When have you seen the temptation of pride bring failure to a ministry? (pp. 21-22) How can you protect yourself from becoming proud as you have success in ministry? (pp. 22-24)

8. In Joseph's response to his brothers, how can we see that he has become a mature leader? (p. 20)

9. Why was the healing of childhood memories necessary for Joseph to be an effective leader? (pp. 23-25) How did healing take place? (p. 24)

10. How does Joseph show that he has developed a God-centered outlook? (pp. 22-25)

11. Have you ever known a leader who had this kind of God-centered approach to ministry? Describe that person.

# 2

# INADEQUACY

## Moses

Aт FIRST SIGHT MOSES COULD APPEAR TO BE A STUDY IN CON-
tradictions. In Exodus 2, when we first meet him in his adult
years, we see him kill an Egyptian in a fit of temper. In the next
chapter we watch him making excuse after excuse as he tries
to avoid a difficult assignment God has given him. And then we
find the same man described as "very meek, more than all men
that were on the face of the earth" (Num 12:3 RSV). So he was
meek, yet possessed a temper which could involve him in man-
slaughter, and at the same time he did his best to dodge when
faced with a demanding task. What common feature is there in
all this variety of behavior and character? It is surely an underlying sense of inadequacy.

## A Common Experience among Church Leaders

Spiritual leadership, if undertaken conscientiously, can expose inadequacy in any of us because of the great demands it makes. This ought not to surprise us because the Bible clearly shows that God does not use superhumans for his work, but ordinary human beings who share our common weaknesses. Among those who stand out as leaders in the Bible, Moses is by no means alone in feeling insufficient for the demands being placed upon him. There was Gideon who, when God called him to be a national deliverer, countered with the objection, "My clan is the weakest in Manasseh, and I am the least in my family" (Judg 6:15). Isaiah could speak only of the moral failings in his life which seemed to disqualify him from being a prophet who could expose the sins of others. Jeremiah thought that his youth would bar him from fulfilling the task being laid before him: " 'Ah, Sovereign LORD,' I said, 'I do not know how to speak; I am only a child' " (Jer 1:6). Perhaps even young Joseph, had he known what God had ultimately in store for him, would not have been quite so ready to recount his youthful dreams.

Faced with sufficient demands, even the strongest and most capable can feel inadequate. If Moses had been left to a private life of comfort in Midian looking after his father-in-law's sheep, he may well have felt quite sufficient for his tasks. Even if he had chosen to stay on in Pharaoh's palace, he might not have been aware of any inadequacy. Josephus and other extrabiblical records tell of his achievements both as a statesman and as a soldier. Indeed, with Joseph's attainments as a precedent, who can tell what heights he might have risen to? But he denounced it all. Instead he "refused to be known as the son of Pharaoh's daughter. He chose to be mistreated along with the people of God rather than to enjoy the pleasures of sin for a short time"

(Heb 11:24-25). First, he turned his back on the sensuality of Pharaoh's court, denouncing his prospects of worldly advancement in Egypt. After he took his part with the Hebrew slaves and then later the call to lead them out of Egypt in the teeth of Pharaoh's military might, he was confronted with a challenge which could well have made the stoutest of hearts tremble.

When, in Exodus 2, Moses surveys the plight of God's people, he immediately has a foretaste of the two directions from which the heavy demands upon him were to come. They are the same for church leaders in any age. First he had to face the challenge of an antagonistic world. At this stage in his life it was the might of Egypt represented here by the Egyptian who was ill-treating a Hebrew slave. His conflict with the world did not end when he left Egypt at the head of Israel on their way to the Promised Land. There were other enemies with which to reckon and always the inhospitable conditions of the desert.

Even today in times of persecution by unfriendly governments it is usually leaders who are picked on. The media can be merciless in their treatment of church leaders, scrutinizing their opinions, sometimes holding them up to ridicule—and the failures of Christian leaders usually provide a real field day! Many of us can echo the complaint of Cardinal Heenan that some parts of the press made him "feel like the captain of a team whose matches are reported only when it loses or has players sent off the field."[1]

We read of how the next day Moses had the first hint of the other source of his coming trials—the people of Israel. As a foretaste, Moses experienced the ingratitude, rejection and disloyalty of the Hebrew whom he aided the previous day. Perhaps the most hurtful aspect of the whole episode was the way Moses' leadership was rejected with the words, "Who made you ruler and judge over us?" (Ex 2:14).

Moses discovered again how difficult the people could be when his first approach to Pharaoh only made matters worse, and the foremen of Israel vented their feelings on him and Aaron. When they reached the Red Sea and panicked at the discovery that the Egyptian army was at their heels, it was Moses who was at the receiving end of their wrath. All through the forty years of wandering in the desert, whenever anything went wrong it was Moses who was blamed.

A Christian minister must always be prepared for this kind of treatment and to be blamed for any failure in a church's work. Lack of response to evangelism and absence of growth in church membership are assumed, as often as not, to be his fault. As Sir John Betjeman said:

When things go wrong it's rather tame
To find we are ourselves to blame;
It gets the trouble over quicker
To go and blame things on the Vicar.

### Coping with Inadequacy

Moses' first attempt at relieving the suffering of his compatriots was a disaster. At the sight of an Egyptian ill-treating a Hebrew, he lost his temper and killed him. It resulted in Moses having to flee the country. Where did he go wrong? He made the mistake of allowing his emotions to control him and the feelings of the moment to determine a course of action. In his case it was the emotion of anger.

Now there is nothing wrong with anger in itself because, like any other human emotion, it is God-given. Jesus, the perfect human, displayed it when the occasion demanded. Moses too had every reason to be indignant at the cruel treatment being meted out to a defenseless slave. But he should never have allowed his feelings of rage to dominate him and decide such a disastrous course of action. This is when, to use the words of James, "man's anger does not bring about the righteous life that God desires" (Jas 1:20). Nor is uncontrolled emotion in keeping with the life of faith in God. Hebrews 11 includes Moses in its list of Old Testament people of faith. Although Moses achieved much "by faith" (Heb 11:23-29), we are not told that by faith he killed the Egyptian. Instead the Old Testament historian, presumably Moses himself, describes how he looked "this way and that and seeing no one, he killed the Egyptian" (Ex 2:12).

Domination by one's emotions is neither the way of faith nor is it spiritual. This needs stressing in these days when it is fashionable to believe what one feels to be true and behave in the way one feels to be right. Many Christians assume that following their feelings is spiritual and the way of guidance. The tragedy is that when we fail to use our minds and instead rely upon our feelings, it is not the Holy Spirit who takes over but our flesh with its weaknesses. The Holy Spirit and the mind of a Christian have an important factor in common—they share the same foe, the flesh. "I myself in my mind am a slave to God's law, but in the sinful nature a slave to the law of sin," writes Paul in Romans 7:25, and in Galatians 5:16 he describes the same conflict as it occurs between the Spirit and the flesh.

Christian leaders need to exercise special care in this area. The work they direct is in real danger if their decisions are based on the feelings of the moment, and their emotional reaction to the pressures on them. It is always unwise to immediately mail a letter which was written in a moment of anger. Far better is it to a sleep on it and read it again in the following morning before sending it. Nor should we pick up the telephone immediately after being provoked. Here is a piece of good advice typical of the book of Proverbs, "Good sense makes a man slow to anger" (Prov 19:11 RSV).

Moses demonstrates that loss of temper can often arise out of a failure to handle our feeling of inadequacy. To use Pauline language, it is when we speak "according to the sinful nature" instead of "according to the Spirit" (Rom 8:4). The weaknesses of our fallen human nature include inadequacy, insecurity, sensitivity and so on. It accounted for the failure of the disciples in the Garden of Gethsemane showing, as Jesus—pointed out to them, that "the spirit is willing, but the flesh is weak" (Mt 26:41). The sin within us (Rom 7:17) will exploit those weaknesses when we speak from our sinful nature.

An angry outburst is a sign that we cannot cope, and is a fleshly and futile way of trying to overcome our failure. Because a person feels incapable of clear self-expression, a friendly discussion between Christians can develop into a heated argument in which tempers are frayed. For the same reason, a tired and harassed mother can lose her temper with the children she dearly loves. Again, it is an inability to cope, and tiredness can make an extra contribution.

Moses made the same mistake many years later when the Israelites were approaching very near to the Promised Land. The rebellious crowd, who had tried his patience so often before, grumbled about a water shortage. In a rage he disobeyed God and struck the rock from which they were to obtain water instead of just speaking to it as God had instructed him. Alexander Whyte made the following pertinent comment: "Moses struck the rock that late day with the very same stroke of angry passion with which he had killed the Egyptian in that early day."[2]

Uncontrolled angry passion is not the only result of an inadequate person walking according to sinful nature. In Exodus 3 we see Moses advancing his inadequacy as a reason for declining God's call to challenge the might of Pharaoh and lead

Israel out of Egypt. It may seem an attractive expression of humility, but God did not regard it so, for "the LORD's anger burned against Moses" (Ex 4:14). This was after God had assured Moses with the promise of his presence and revealed himself in his name, "I AM WHO I AM" (Ex 3:14). When, in the face of the promises of God and the great truths he has revealed of himself, we persist in advancing our insufficiency as an excuse for avoiding our responsibilities, it is a mark not of humility but of unbelief.

All this, however, is not the whole truth about Moses. We later see this timid man fearlessly challenge Pharaoh and lead God's people out of Egypt. When hemmed in by the Red Sea before him and Pharaoh's army in hot pursuit behind him, he calmed the situation as he reassured his distracted followers, "Do not be afraid. Stand firm and you will see the deliverance the LORD will bring you today" (Ex 14:13). Throughout the forty years in the desert, Moses was in command of the situation as he brought the Israelites through many a crisis. At the same time, there was no seeking after vain glory. After Israel had turned to idolatry, God declared his intention to give up Israel, but said to Moses, "Then I will make you into a great nation" (Ex 32:10). Moses declined the offer, even though it had come from God himself. His supreme concern was not personal ambition, but God's glory and the good of his people. What had happened to Moses—this inadequate man who now combined courage with self-effacement? Had he ceased to be inadequate? The difference was that he regarded his inadequacy as reason for trusting in the Lord. In Paul's terms, this is what happens when an inadequate person "walks after the Spirit."

Paul had a similar experience of having the Spirit of God use his fleshly weaknesses. He describes how his ministry in Corinth had been "in weakness and fear, and with much trembling," but at the same time was "with a demonstration of the Spirit's power" (1 Cor 2:3-4). But this salutary awareness of his weakness did not always come naturally to Paul, as he reveals in 2 Corinthians 12. There, he refers to a time when, because of a special revelation he had received, he had been in danger of "becoming conceited because of these surpassingly great revelations" (v. 7). Even the great apostle was not immune to spiritual pride. To prevent this from happening Paul continues, "there was given me a thorn in my flesh, a messenger of Satan, to torment me" (v. 7). Whatever it was, it was a fleshly weakness and Satanic in origin and Paul assumed he would be better off without it. So there were three occasions when he asked God to remove it (v. 8). But God thought otherwise and instead gave him the promise, "My grace is sufficient for you, for my power is made perfect in weakness" (v. 9). His weakness, under God, became a means of grace through which he was able to prove his power, and he was able to testify, "Therefore I will boast all the more gladly about my weaknesses, so that Christ's power may rest on me. . . . For when I am weak, then am I strong" (vv. 9-10). Moses made the same discovery.

After fleeing from Egypt, Moses spent forty years in the desert of Midian as a shepherd. We are not told much about those years, but solitude seems to have played an important part in the early preparation of many of God's leaders. Paul, for example, spent a number of years alone in the Arabian desert before he set out on his life's work. We are, however, given the details of an important event which changed the whole direction of Moses' life. It was his encounter with God at the burning bush on Mount Sinai.

### Three Lessons for an Inadequate Person
When God spoke to Moses from the burning bush (Ex 3—4),

and called him to return to Egypt, confront Pharaoh and lead the Israelites out of slavery to Canaan, his lack of enthusiasm for the idea is hardly to be wondered at. After all, the circumstances in which he had previously left Egypt were not such as to encourage him to return as a national deliverer. In any case why leave Midian where he was nicely settled as a family man and manager of his father-in-law's sheep farm, an occupation well within his ability? But there were a number of important lessons for Moses to learn.

The first lesson was to humble himself before God. This may sound surprising because lessons in humility seem hardly needed by someone who is inadequate and knows it. But regarding oneself as a complete failure is not the same thing as being humble before God. Professor J. D. Mackenzie has drawn this distinction: "Humiliation makes a man look down on himself, whereas true humility makes the individual look up to God."[3] It is humility which is essential if our weakness is to cast us back on the strength of God. This is clearly Peter's understanding of humility when he writes: "All of you, clothe yourselves with humility toward one another, because 'God opposes the proud, but gives grace to the humble.' Humble yourselves, therefore, under God's mighty hand, that he may lift you up in due time" (1 Pet 5:5-6).

Such an attitude toward God needed to be informed by three vital truths. First Moses had to recognize that he was face to face with the living God, described by R. T. France as "a God to be reckoned with." What attracted Moses' attention to the bush was "that though the bush was on fire it did not burn up" (Ex 3:2), a fitting manifestation of the One who is self-sufficient, dependent on no one and never changes. This truth was made explicit through the name by which God revealed himself to Moses, "I AM WHO I AM" (v. 14). Shortened, this clause becomes

JHWH, the characteristic name for God in the Old Testament. A complete discussion of the meaning and use of this name is beyond our scope here. We content ourselves by noting that the verb *to be* at its heart denotes something much more than mere existence. As R. T. France summarizes it, " 'To be' in Hebrew means an active, dynamic presence."[5] It was also conveyed by the formula "as the LORD lives," which the prophets used to affirm that God is ready and able to carry out the word they were about to declare.

The burning bush also spoke of God's moral excellence and purity, as fire always did when associated with God. It expressed God's protest against the sin of humanity at his expulsion from the Garden of Eden when "he placed on the east side of the Garden of Eden cherubim and a flaming sword flashing back and forth to guard the way to the tree of life" (Gen 3:24). Moses had to realize that by nature he was unfit for contact with such a God until he had taken certain ceremonial precautions: "Do not come any closer. . . . Take off your sandals for the place where you are standing is holy ground" (v. 5).

The voice from the burning bush then revealed to Moses the third truth he needed to know—that the living and holy God who was confronting him was not some distant deity, but the God of Moses' own people. He said, "I am the God of your father, the God of Abraham, the God of Isaac and the God of Jacob" (v. 6).

Moses' reaction was one of reverence and awe. He "hid his face, because he was afraid to look at God" (v. 6). Here is the secret of the spiritual strength which transformed Moses' debilitating low self-image into a humble dependence upon God. It was this trust that helped him to stand fearlessly before Pharaoh proving that in "the fear of the LORD one has strong confidence" (Prov 14:26 RSV).

Moses had run away from Egypt out of fear. A fear of humanity is a common problem and needs to be replaced by a reverential fear of God. As Tate and Beady expressed it in their well-known paraphrase of Psalm 34, "Fear Him, ye saints; and you will then have nothing else to fear." It seems that Lord Napier, a British field marshall in India during the 19th century, knew this secret, judging from his epitaph in Westminster Abbey, "He feared men so little, because he feared God so much."

Another help in coping with inadequacy is a strong conviction that we are in the place of God's choosing. When our work is difficult, our Christian service is not meeting with the success we would like, and we become conscious of our limitations, it is all too easy to long for other spheres of service which appear to match our limited capabilities. If we then entertain doubts about whether we have been mistaken in our guidance and are in the wrong place, this can undermine us further, and the grass on the other side of the fence looks even greener. No doubt Moses, when his first encounters with Pharaoh did not meet with immediate success, could have thought of other tasks in which he would have been much more successful. One of Paul's encouragements to perseverance is the promise, "In due season we shall reap, if we do not lose heart" (Gal 6:9). But such a promise is undermined if we are not sure that we are where God wants us to be. Moses, however, persevered because he was unshaken in his conviction that it was God who had sent him to Pharaoh. And he received this conviction at the burning bush.

God's purpose for Moses was first revealed in his perfect knowledge of the situation. So God began by assuring him, "I have indeed seen the misery of my people" (v. 7). Moreover he understood the plight of his people as he continued: "I have heard them crying out . . . I am concerned about their suffering." Moses was about to be commissioned by a God who was well acquainted with the needs of his people and deeply enraged about their trials. It was then that God unveiled his plan "to rescue them from the hand of the Egyptians" (v. 8).

The most unexpected part of God's plan was the human instrument chosen to bring it about. He said to Moses, "I am sending you" (v. 10). Moses thought he was the last one who should be chosen for such a daunting task; his last memory of Egypt was his pathetic attempt all those years ago to help one of his oppressed countrymen. Yet the Bible shows how God uses inadequate people who make an unpromising start. Who would have thought that Joseph, the boy with egocentric dreams, pampered by his father and despised by his brothers, could have such a significant role to play in Egypt? David was hardly the most obvious choice for a future king, when even his own father did not think he was worth presenting to Samuel, yet he became the greatest monarch in Old Testament history. An obvious exception was Paul who had risen to some prominence before his conversion, but he was an exception, as most of the other church leaders had been described as "uneducated, common men" (Acts 4:13 RSV). Moses, in spite of his advantage of an education in Pharaoh's household, and the positions he had already held in Egypt, did not regard himself as a natural choice for God's purpose. Yet it was made quite clear that God had appointed him to leadership and this conviction remained with him throughout his struggle with Pharaoh and the frustrations of the long years in the desert.

The largest part of the account of Moses at the burning bush is devoted to the third answer to Moses' inadequacy—the sufficiency of God for every demand he makes of us. This was given to Moses as answers to four excuses he advanced, obstacles which seemed to him to stand in the way of God's plan for him.

Moses' first excuse was simply the problem of himself, "Who am I that I should go?" (Ex 3:11). God's reply was equally simple, "I will be with you" (v. 12). Simple though it is, in this statement is the perfect match to our weaknesses. It is the answer to Christians who never open their mouths in testimony out of fear that they may put up a poor performance. It invalidates this kind of excuse for avoiding positions of responsibility in one's church.

The celebrated violinist Paganini provided Victorian preachers with a number of illustrations. One was the occasion when he was reputed to have broken three of the four strings on his violin at a concert. For some reason he had no replacements with him. So he continued to play on one string, and although this obviously restricted him, he was still able to produce music of a high standard.

Inadequate people may feel like the violin with only one string. In the hands of the Master, however, there is the possibility of fruitful service. Indeed, taking the illustration further, it is far better to be like the violin with one string played by Paganini, than like a four-stringed instrument in other hands. So the vital question is not "How adequate am I?" but "Am I completely in the Master's hands?"

Then Moses advanced his second excuse, "Suppose I go to the Israelites and say to them, 'The God of your fathers has sent me to you,' and they ask me, 'What is his name?' what shall I tell them?" (v. 13). One cannot avoid having some sympathy with Moses at this point. He is rightly reluctant to assume leadership of God's people ill-equipped. He sees the need to be able to answer their questions. So God reminds Moses that he has not left his people to speculate and guess, but has revealed himself to the founding fathers of the Old Testament church, Abraham, Isaac and Jacob. And it did not end there because God added, "This is my name forever, the name by which I am to be remembered from generation to generation" (v. 15). And he was indeed remembered by future generations as the revelation was passed on from one generation to another.

Today church members still expect their leaders to be able to answer their questions. Pastors in some parts of the world are finding this especially demanding where their young people are receiving a better education than they did. Like Moses, they ask or ought to ask "What shall I say to them?" And the answer is still basically the same as that given to Moses.

Christianity is a revealed religion. It is not the product of religious geniuses finding their way to God, but is the result of God supernaturally revealing himself, as he has done supremely through Jesus Christ. If Christian leaders are to exercise ministry with confidence, they need to master the truth God has revealed. In other words they must know the Bible, the truth it contains and why it is inspired and completely reliable. If there is any truth in Francis Bacon's claim that "knowledge is power," then a knowledge of God's Word can bring confidence to any Christian (always remembering the warning of 1 Corinthians 8:1 that was addressed to Christians who were not especially conscious of any inadequacy!).

Moses' third excuse was to express his concern whether the Israelites would accept his leadership. Here is a question which at least crosses the mind of most leaders when undertaking a new sphere of work and can be expressed in many different ways: "What will my new congregation think of me? How can I make a favorable impression on them? How will they compare me with my predecessor?" I once discovered how a well-known evangelist was in bondage to anxieties of this kind, when a

Christian leader confided to me how the evangelist frequently asked him what his public image was like. Moses was bothered by such questions and did not highly assess his chances of being accepted. The extent of his expectation was simply "What if they do not believe me or listen to me?" (4:1).

To overcome his misgivings Moses was given power to perform three supernatural signs. For the Hebrews Moses was to lead, these signs would have special weight, surrounded as they were by Egyptian magic. But how do we apply this today? Those who believe that signs and wonders are to be expected as a normal experience for us, as they were for the apostles, will have a simple answer to such a question, but what about the rest of us who are not so sure about such theories? Surely the answer is that the power to work miracles is not the only equipment which God provides for his servants. There are many gifts which the Holy Spirit in his wisdom gives, and just as Moses was furnished with all that he needed for his ministry to God's people in the Middle East of his day, so we can trust God to do the same for us in the last part of the twentieth century. If we are serving God in the place of his choosing, we may rest assured that he never sends us to a task without the necessary gifts. Here is the timeless principle which ought to displace all worries about what people think of us.

Moses' fourth and final excuse shows that he had not completely grasped the above principle because he confessed his worries about his lack of gifts for speech, "I have never been eloquent, neither in the past nor since you have spoken to your servant. I am slow of speech and tongue" (4:10). This could indicate not only that Moses regarded himself as a poor speaker, but that he suffered from a speech defect such as stammering. This is a real possibility since stammering often accompanies feelings of inferiority. Indeed the sufferers find themselves in a vicious circle, since their stammering makes them feel all the more inadequate. Perhaps Moses anticipated that if the Israelites threw doubts on his credentials, his increased feelings of diffidence could only make his stammering worse. And then what about facing Pharaoh, who may well have regarded him as a despised Hebrew when they were boys together in the royal palace? Here is a situation which a stammerer could hardly relish. It may be that Moses' reference, "since you have spoken to your servant," meant that he had been stammering during the course of his conversation with God, and this would indicate how Moses reacted to stress.

Relaxation plays an important part in the treatment of this condition and this is aided by building up the sufferer's confidence. Hence the appropriateness of God's simple promise, "I will help you speak and will teach you what to say" (4:12). If Moses could be assured of a close relationship between God and his speech, this in itself could reduce tension. Nor is the additional pledge to "teach you what you shall speak" without significance. Uncertainty about what to say could be an additional hazard for a stammerer.

Moses, however, was still not ready to submit himself completely to God's will, so he made one further attempt to avoid the challenge before him, "Oh, Lord, please send someone else to do it" (v. 13). God, who had shown much patience with Moses, was not angry. Yet, at the same time, he agreed to send Aaron, adding, "I know he can speak well" (v. 14). He was not, however, to be a substitute for Moses, but a companion.

Here is a fruitful area for study in the life of Moses. A feeling of inadequacy sometimes causes persons in leadership positions to reject help from those gifted in the very skills which they lack. Fearful of showing up their own limitations, they see the prospect of gifted support as a threat to their own security.

Insisting that they need to know how to do any job better than their subordinates, they pass over well-qualified people and select instead those who have little to add to their own contribution. Such can be the defense mechanism of an inferiority complex.

Although Moses readily accepted the help of Aaron (at that stage he was prepared to grasp at any straw), he had not yet learned this lesson. Some years later his father-in-law, Jethro, saw that the burden of office in the wilderness was proving a great strain. Jethro could see that his son-in-law was undertaking far too much and in danger of wearing himself out. He suggested that Moses should delegate some of his judicial authority to others and have only the hard cases brought directly to himself. Happily, Moses was by now ready to accept this advice (Ex 18:13).

The calling and service of Moses were, of course, exceptional. But they have much to teach any of us troubled by feelings of inadequacy, however lowly our own leadership position may be by comparison. In church, business, government, home, family, to name but a few examples, many a personal failure, and many a corporate failure too, might have been avoided by learning and applying the lessons from such relevant Bible history. In a key New Testament passage, Paul reminds us that the gifts of God are diverse, "It was he who gave some to be apostles, some to be prophets, some to be evangelists, and some to be pastors and teachers" (Eph 4:11). So where we are lacking, we may look to God to supply the need through someone else.

Then there is the need for fellowship. The problems of inadequate persons are intensified if they are isolated. It is worth noting that Moses and Aaron are not the only pair in Scripture to team up together. The New Testament has a number of examples, such as Peter and John, Paul and Barnabas, Paul and

Silas, Barnabas and Mark, and the seventy disciples whom Jesus sent out in twos.

It ought to be emphasized that what we learn from God's treatment of Moses does not merely supplement the psychological approach in vogue today, but flatly contradicts much of it. It is the assumption that what is needed for effective Christian leadership is to build up one's self-esteem. What is essential, however, is God's presence with us—as he promised it to Moses (Ex 3:12). We must not ignore God's power while focusing on personal emotional problems.

**The Making of a Leader**
Stripped of all excuses, and with the promises and provision of God which more than answered them, Moses submitted himself to God's will and set off for Egypt, accompanied by wife and family. He was given the assurance that those who had sought his life when he had made his hurried exit from Egypt were now dead (Ex 4:19). He duly met Aaron and shared with him the instructions he had received. On arrival in Egypt they assembled the elders, Aaron addressed them, and Moses made use of the miraculous signs he had been given. Their initial response could not have been more encouraging (4:27-31).

So far, so good. They now had to meet Pharaoh. Moses had already been warned that this would be a tough assignment and that Pharaoh would harden his heart. Indeed, their first encounter with Pharaoh was a disaster. Instead of letting the Israelites go, he stepped up the pressure on them. The reaction of the Israelites was predictable. They decided to send their own deputation to Pharaoh, and when this was no more successful than the attempt of Moses and Aaron, they turned on them. It is easy to imagine how Moses felt when he said: "O LORD, why have you brought trouble upon this people? Is this why you sent me? Ever since I went to Pharaoh to speak in your name, he has brought trouble upon this people, and you have not rescued your people at all" (5:22-23).

It is natural to sympathize with Moses. Surely, if there was one thing that this inadequate man needed at this stage, it was some success in establishing his leadership to give him confidence. Isn't this one of the reasons why every leader needs success? Here is where it is all too easy to misunderstand the ways of God. In the short term an early victory over Pharaoh would certainly have enhanced Moses' reputation with the Israelites. God, however, was looking further ahead to the tremendous demands that were to be made of Moses and for that he would need to be a spiritual giant. We do not underestimate what happened to Moses at the burning bush, but it was only a turning point, decisive though it proved to be. The work of sanctification for God's people—whether leaders or not—does not come about through one crisis experience, but is a process. For Moses, as for Joseph, this involved practical training in a tough school. It meant hard work with Pharaoh. But in the course of it, a spiritual calibre and authority soon began to appear in the boldness with which he addressed Pharaoh. What became of his speech difficulties which Aaron was supposed to help with? We are given no explicit answer to this question, but we may draw our own conclusions from the way that Aaron seems to slip into the background.

Most important of all, by the time they left Egypt, Moses had established himself as leader of Israel. He had to endure their unbelief, grumblings, panic, ungodliness and their constant readiness to blame him for every setback that befell them. Yet in all this, Moses endured as a person of faith who never lost his conviction about the great destiny to which God was leading them. Again and again, he stood like a tower among them.

Once more, Rudyard Kipling in his poem *If* provides us with words to describe the maturity of a person of God:

If you can keep your head when all about you

Are losing theirs and blaming it on you . . .

Yours is the earth and everything that's in it,

And—which is more—you'll be a man my son.

What had happened to Moses' inadequacy? Had he lost it and become a self-assured, insensitive extrovert who knew how to dominate those under him? Not according to the following description of him, "Now Moses was a very humble man, more humble than anyone else on the face of the earth" (Num 12:3). The occasion on which that was said of Moses is instructive. It was when he met a direct challenge to his leadership from his own flesh and blood, Miriam and Aaron—a severe test for anyone with a basic feeling of insecurity. Moses' leadership could well have collapsed in the face of it or he could have flown into a rage. Instead the Bible simply draws attention to his meekness and shows how God vindicated Moses' leadership.

There are two prayers on the lips of Moses which reveal something of the kind of leader he had become. The first shows he had allowed his inadequacy to lead to a distrust of himself which was accompanied by a dependence on God: "If your Presence does not go with us, do not send us up from here" (Ex 33:15). In spite of all his achievements and the difficulties he had overcome, he was still conscious of his insufficiency and need of the presence of God. The other prayer follows a few verses later: "Now show me your glory" (Ex 33:18).

He might well have sought some kind of aggrandizement to compensate for his inferiority feelings, but such thoughts were far from his mind. Instead the desire of his heart was to know God more deeply and in fuller measure. It is aspirations like this which are the making of a leader with spiritual authority.

Moses' request could not be fully met during this life, but he received a remarkable answer. God's glory was reflected in Moses himself. He was called up Mount Sinai to receive a second copy of the Ten Commandments. As he came down from the mountain, this is what happened, "Moses did not know that the skin of his face shone because he had been talking with God" (Ex 34:29 RSV).

This was a foretaste of what was in store for Moses beyond the grave. He may have been excluded from the Promised Land, but along with Elijah, he was to share in the glory which Jesus knew on the Mount of Transfiguration. But to return to earth, note the significant feature of the glory displayed in the shining of Moses' face. He was unaware of it himself. How different from some "spiritual" but, one suspects, inadequate Christians who can never cease from talking about some "higher life" experience, which marks them out from other more ordinary believers. It is all very immature, like the little girl who keeps saying "Look at my pretty dress." Moses' concern, like all those who have trodden the same path, was not with himself and the impression he was making, but with the glory of God. This is the maturity to which God calls every inadequate Christian.

## Questions for Individuals or Groups

1. What are some of the reasons that the author gives for feelings of inadequacy in biblical leaders? (pp. 28-29) Why might leaders today feel inadequate for the task that God has called them to?

2. The author mentions that the incident with the Egyptian gave Moses' a foretaste of the pressures that would be placed upon him from two different sources. (pp. 29-30) What were these? What are the sources of pressure that leaders face today? (p. 30)

3. Moses killed the Egyptian out of anger. (p. 30) When have you seen a leader or a ministry injured because of unguarded anger?

4. What does the author sight as the causes of Moses' angry outbursts with the Egyptian and the Israelites? (pp. 31-32)

5. Why does the Lord become angry with Moses? (pp. 33-34)

6. What did Moses learn about God at the burning bush? (pp. 35-36) What effect did each of these facts have upon Moses?

7. How did knowing God's purpose for him help Moses to cope with his inadequacy? (pp. 37-38)

8. What excuses did Moses make to try to escape God's command? (pp. 39-43) How did God discount each of Moses' responses?

9. What excuses do we give God today?

10. Why is it significant that Moses willingly accepted Aaron's help? (pp. 42-43)

11. Why do you think that Moses was not granted an early victory with Pharaoh? (pp. 44-45)

12. How does Moses' inadequacy develop into the positive quality of humility as he matures? (pp. 45-47)

13. What specific encouragement does Moses' story give you as you grow as a leader?

# 3

# SEXUAL TEMPTATION

## Samson, David, Solomon

COPING WITH OUR SEXUALITY IS A NECESSITY FOR EVERY CHRIStian leader and yet we look in vain for a particular Bible character to help us. This is because, unlike the topics of our other chapters such as immaturity, depression and sensitivity which affect different people in varying degrees, sex is common to all, and the leaders in the Bible are no exception. Just because many of them got through their lives without having either any lapse recorded of them or any occasion when they were victorious in this realm mentioned, does not mean that they never had any problems. Because they were all truly human, possessing bodies with the same biology as anyone else, they all had to cope with their sexuality, the vast majority of them successfully.

We have seen how Joseph was put to the test, and his example shows how it is possible to come through the strongest
temptation unscathed. In this chapter, on the other hand, we
will look at three examples of failure, which serve as warnings.

**Samson**
From the account of his life in the book of Judges it is apparent
that he had many achievements as he championed the cause
of Israel against their archenemy, the Philistines. He even
made the honors list in Hebrews 11, although his is only a
passing reference. But it is also patently obvious that his life fell
a long way short of what it might have been. J. Oswald Sanders
has a chapter about him entitled, "The Champion who became
a clown,"[1] no doubt referring to the degrading way he ended
his life in the Philistine stadium. The chief cause of his downfall was the succession of involvements with undesirable Philistine women which marred his life.

He began full of promise with everything going for him. He
had the advantage of godly parents to whom it was revealed
that he would be a Nazarite. This meant that he would vow to
abstain from the fruit of the vine, leave his hair uncut and
refrain from any contact with the dead. All this would express
his consecration to God for the very special task to which God
had called him—to "begin the deliverance of Israel from the
hands of the Philistines" (Judg 13:5) who were oppressing Israel at that time. His consecration to God, together with absti-
nence from some sensual enjoyments, was the secret of the
outstanding physical strength with which the Spirit of God
endued him and for which he has ever since been renowned.
As he grew up, "the Lord blessed him" (Judg 13:24) and, at an
early age the Spirit of the Lord "began to drive him hard" (Judg
13:25 NEB).

Then came the first of his unfortunate liaisons with the opposite sex. When Sampson was barely out of his teens, an attractive Philistine young woman took his fancy, and he went
home and announced to his parents his intention to marry her.
It happened so quickly that it was probably little more than
physical attraction. His godly parents were understandably distressed that their son, for whom they were sure God had great
purposes, should set his affection on a pagan girl. Subsequent
events proved that she was indeed an unsatisfactory partner.

This has a familiar ring to it. We think of the young people
from Christian homes who play a leading part in the church.
Their strong orthodox opinions, tinged perhaps with characteristic teen-age arrogance, and enthusiasm for Christian work,
seem to be evidence that the Holy Spirit is "driving them hard."
Then, without any warning (it seems), a non-Christian member
of the opposite sex takes their fancy, and in a short time their
Christian testimony becomes sadly diminished. We learn what
an effective weapon sexual attraction can be in the hands of
the devil. Those called to full-time Christian service are exposed to this danger as much as anyone, and there are many
whose ministries have been sadly impaired by an unsuitable
partner.

Even though this fell a long way short of the best, here is one
of those occasions when God shows his sovereignty in a remarkable way. If we find it difficult to comprehend, then so
must Samson's parents, for we are told that his "parents did not
know that this was from the LORD, who was seeking an occasion
to confront the Philistines" (Judg 14:4). Through God's overruling, the affair came to nothing, as the Philistine girl's disloyalty
toward Samson showed that her pagan standards were far lower than those under which he had been brought up. Sadly,
Sampson failed to learn from this incident to beware of such

women of the world and to protect his vulnerability.

The biblical narrative proceeds to recount Samson's achievements, noting occasions when he broke his Nazarite vow. After involvement with a prostitute at Gaza, from which again he learned nothing, he became infatuated with Delilah, an episode which proved to be the greatest tragedy of all.

Something of Samson's worth as an Israelite leader is seen by the way the Philistines still regarded him as a threat. Delilah fell for the bribe they offered and used her seductive powers to discover the secret of Samson's strength (Judg 16:1-19). He was so blinded by passion that he failed to see through her hypocrisy. It is true he did not succumb easily, but she persisted day after day, using all the emotional blackmail she could think of until she eventually succeeded, and Samson's career as a leader was over.

When Samson was warned by Delilah, as he had been before, of the approach of the Philistines, he rose to meet them unaware of what had happened. "He did not know that the LORD had left him" (Judg 16:20). Thus, A. E. Cundall says "there is possibly no sadder verse in the Old Testament."[2] Samson was disgraced, but worst of all the name of Jehovah was dishonored in favor of the Philistine idol Dagon. At the rally called to celebrate, Samson was able to rectify the situation, but it involved ending his own life in suicide.

### David

According to Charles Spurgeon, the earlier part of David's life was full of music and dancing; the latter part had far more of mourning and lamentation in it. What was it that divided David's life into such contrasting parts? It was a sexual scandal. He first committed adultery. That was followed by a pathetic and unsuccessful attempt at a cover-up, and when that failed, he resorted to the murder of the young woman's husband.

How he lived with his conscience during the ensuing months is hard to imagine. He describes his bitter experience in Psalm 32. Eventually, in response to the ministry of the prophet Nathan, he confessed his sin, repented and received an assurance of forgiveness. David said to Nathan, "I have sinned against the Lord." And Nathan said to David, "The Lord has taken away your sin. You are not going to die" (2 Sam 12:13).

It is the word that follows which Spurgeon was drawing attention as being particularly significant—"nevertheless" or "howbeit" in the older version that Spurgeon was using. Although David was forgiven, his life and reign from then on were never the same. Nathan warned him, "This is what the LORD says: "Out of your own household I am going to bring calamity upon you" (2 Sam 12:11) predicting, debauchery within his own family which the whole nation would know about. One has only to recall the names of Tamar, Amnon and Absalom, the latter being David's own son who led an attempted coup d'etat against him, to realize how tragically true Nathan's prediction proved to be. He was like Esau, who sold his birthright to satisfy the carnal desires of the moment.

It would be an exaggeration to pretend that when a Christian leader today falls in the same way, the consequences are always on the same scale. There is, however, ample ground for maintaining that a leader's life and work will probably never be the same after he or she has been at the center of a sexual scandal. One reason is that although when God forgives he forgets, human beings rarely can. In well-known cases the media will often see to it that the memory is kept alive, sometimes for many years after it happened.

David's case warns us that godly men are not immune. The one who indulged himself with a married woman was the writer of many of the Psalms which, when translated, are among the greatest expressions of prayer, praise and worship in the English language. He had many fine qualities. For example, he did not lack courage. When he was trying to persuade Saul to let him go and fight Goliath, he described how he had taken on a lion and bear who had molested his father's flocks. After he had successfully fought with Goliath, he became a popular figure, especially with the girls who sang his praises. After he was anointed king by the prophet Samuel, four times his life was threatened by Saul whom he was due to replace. Yet on two occasions, when he had the opportunity to kill Saul, who was hunting him, he proved to be a person of principle by refusing to take the law into his own hands. Above all, he was described as a man after God's own heart (1 Sam 13:14).

How then did such a person fall? It is true that he had shown a partiality for women in the way that he took advantage of the practice of polygamy which was tolerated in those days. But we have no record of him misbehaving with a married woman until from his rooftop he saw his neighbor, Bathsheba, taking a bath. There are, however, indications that a rot in his character had already begun to set in. To begin with, why wasn't he away leading his armies? Instead he was enjoying the luxuries he had gathered at home in Jerusalem. We are told, "One evening David got up from his bed and walked around on the roof of the palace. From the roof he saw a woman bathing" (2 Sam 11:2). He cannot be criticized for having a siesta—it has always been the usual practice in the early afternoon in a hot Middle Eastern country, but not getting up until evening raises questions. While he cannot be blamed for noticing the woman, what followed was reprehensible and could have been avoided. The result was as tragic as it often is today. It meant the ruin of the rest of his life.

## Solomon

Here is another Old Testament leader who started well. At the very beginning of his reign, his motives were subjected to a searching test when God invited him in a dream to ask for whatever he wanted (1 Kings 3:5). It is not difficult to imagine the kind of thing which the average ruler of those days would have sought. Solomon's answer, however, was based on careful thought. He first looked back to the good example David, his father, had left and thought of the character of God shown in the way he had blessed him. He then made a humble assessment of himself as he confessed, "But I am only a little child and do not know how to go carry out my duties" (3:7). He also showed an encouraging sense of responsibility for the daunting task that lay before him as he opted for "an understanding mind to govern thy people, that I may discern between good and evil" (1 Kings 3:9 RSV). All this boded well for the future. He soon had an opportunity to exercise such discernment when having to adjudicate between two contending women. There were many achievements in his reign, while in his spare time he gave expression to his literary and musical skills by writing 3005 proverbs and composing 1005 Songs (1 Kings 4:32). His reign reached its climax with the dedication of the Temple, and his prayer on that occasion is among the greatest in the Old Testament. His fame spread far and wide and he numbered the Queen of Sheba among his admirers.

At the same time there were ominous indications of a less desirable side to Solomon's character, and the riches he accumulated were of no help to him either morally or spiritually. The real downturn, however, comes in 1 Kings 11 which begins with the revelation that King Solomon "loved many foreign women" (v. 1). The first of a succession of marriages with such women had begun early in his reign when he married the daughter of the Egyptian Pharaoh, but this seems to have been as much a matter of politics as sex. Later, however, it is made clear that he was attracted to them. He "loved" them (1 Kings 11:1). Polygamy was an undesirable practice, although tolerated, but was to be avoided by kings. Among the instructions given through Moses for life in the Promised Land, those given for the king included "he must not take many wives, or his heart will be led astray" (Deut 17:17). And that was exactly what they did for Solomon, for when he "grew old, his wives turned his heart after other gods" (1 Kings 11:4).

The effect of Solomon's bowing to sexual temptation touched the whole kingdom. The trouble with these foreign wives was that, with their background of pagan idolatry, their spiritual outlook was utterly different from that of Israel. Under their influence Solomon was distracted from Jehovah to their gods. When Solomon died, he left behind a population crippled by heavy taxation which, together with slave labor, had been used for the benefit of his lavish projects, such as temples for the gods of his wives.

It is not only polygamists that can be caught in this way. Ministers today can have their work sadly impaired through having a spouse who is spiritually out of tune with them. How is it that gifted evangelicals can get themselves into this position? It is well known how attractive young unmarried ministers can be to the opposite sex in their congregations. In times of loneliness and discouragement, it is all too easy to fall for anyone who shows affection, but may lack a mature relationship with Christ.

We end this chapter on a positive note. The instinct which draws a man and a woman together is part of God's creative purpose and, when under the control of the Holy Spirit, can enrich the lives of us all. Many of those whom God has greatly used would gladly acknowledge what they owe to a satisfying and supportive relationship with their partner. But this instinct is a powerful one and can easily get out of control, as the devil knows well. Here, the teaching of Solomon in the Book of Proverbs is better than his example in 1 Kings and 2 Chronicles. After warning against the loose woman (5:3), the foolish woman (9:13) and the argumentative or ill-tempered woman (21:19), he ends the book with a passage in which he sings the praises of a good wife: "She is worth far more than rubies. Her husband has full confidence in her" (31:10-11). If it is God's will for a person to marry, this is the kind of woman for him! It is a sacred relationship. Let us not allow the devil to spoil it and in the process ruin not only our marriage, but also our ministry.

## Questions for Individuals or Groups

1. What did Sampson's choice of the Philistine woman reveal about him? (pp. 50-51) Explain.

2. Why do you think that Sampson failed to see what Delilah was trying to do? (p. 52)

3. Have you ever known a leader like Sampson? Describe the situation.

4. What were the long term effects of David's sin? (pp. 52-54)

5. When have you seen a Christian leader's sexual sin bring long-term effects to the Christian community? (p. 53) How did non-Christians react?

6. What do you think were the factors in David's life that led to his sin with Bathsheba? (pp. 53-54)

7. How can you protect yourself and your ministry from being in a situation which would allow sexual sin to take place?

8. How did Solomon's polygamous marriages end up being his downfall? (p. 55-56)

9. How was the kingdom affected by Solomon's sin? (p. 56)

10. How is a wisely chosen marriage partner a help in ministry? (pp. 56-57)

11. What qualities do you think are important in a marriage partner?

# 4

# DEPRESSION

## Elijah

ONE OF THE GREATEST CONTRASTS IN THE WHOLE OF SCRIPTURE must be between the picture we get of Elijah in 1 Kings 18 and that which follows in chapter 19. In chapter 18 he stands on Mount Carmel, confidently and victoriously asserting the claims of Jehovah, whereas in the next chapter he is disappointed and disillusioned, writing himself off as a hopeless failure. In the former chapter he fearlessly defies the prophets of Baal and their royal sponsors; we next see him running for his life and fleeing the country.

Depression is a common human problem to which church leaders are not immune. The world has had many examples among its public figures such as political leaders, artists, musicians, poets and writers, while the world of entertainment has produced many cases, including suicides. The church, too, can add many well-known names to the list. Martin Luther knew periods of elation in his life followed by deep depression. Henry Martyn, a much admired missionary pioneer, was subject to bouts of morbid introspection. Some of the hymns of William Cowper reflect his depressive problems which sometimes rendered him suicidal. Charles Spurgeon had his periods of depression which may have been worsened by his suffering from gout.

The Bible also has examples among its most outstanding leaders. There is Job in the Old Testament to put beside Elijah and, judging from what he had to endure, he had cause to be depressed. John the Baptist, who did not shrink from denouncing the errors of his day and dared to rebuke King Herod for his corrupt life, was depressed when in prison. He even questioned the Messiahship of Jesus after all his preaching about him. Paul became depressed and discouraged and on more than one occasion he needed a word of comfort from God (Acts 18:9; 23:11). In his epistles he does not disguise his feeling of distress over the failings in some of the churches he had founded.

Elijah's depression is not what one might expect from his public stance on Mount Carmel. He is like the successful businessperson, who appears to be in complete command of every situation, without any obvious excuse for depression, yet his or her spouse knows well that behind the scenes, he often lives under a cloud. For example I knew an outgoing Christian youth leader, who had led many young people to faith in Christ, and then discovered to my complete surprise, many years later, that he suffered from depression. Some well-known preachers, who have put many of us in their debt, have had to endure the same affliction. A common experience, which is very close to that of

Elijah, is fearlessly to take a stand on some controversial issue and, while in the pulpit, to feel on top of the world, yet afterward to be overwhelmed by regrets and even feelings of guilt. Our study of Elijah ought to give us an insight into the nature of this condition and the Bible's prescription for its treatment.

## The Causes of Depression

Very often there is an obvious cause of depression in a person's circumstances such as family or occupation. Peter anticipates that Christians undergoing earthly trials will sometimes feel mental distress, using a word translated "heaviness" (1 Pet 1:6, KJV), or "grief" (NIV). Elijah had reason enough to feel depressed when he considered the state of Israel. Instead of trying to worship Jehovah in an idolatrous fashion—which had been a temptation ever since Aaron had made the golden calf, thereby breaking the second commandment—they now had broken the first commandment by rejecting God altogether and turning to the heathen god Baal. This was the complaint which Elijah spelled out to God: "I have been very zealous for the LORD God Almighty. The Israelites have rejected your covenant, broken down your altars, and put your prophets to death with the sword" (1 Kings 19:10). He recognized Jehovah's right to be "a jealous God" (Ex 34:14), which is the jealousy of a lover who will not share his beloved with anyone else, and he too was jealous for the Lord. He was like the psalmist who longed that God should preserve his honor by vindicating himself in the face of the blasphemies of godless people (Ps 94:1-3). Jesus, too, showed similar concerns when he wept over the people of Jerusalem.

Who can criticize Elijah or any other leader for being depressed about such a state of affairs? He really cared, and so should we. Unbelievers do not always understand such concerns, and their advice is often not to take things too seriously, labelling such a person a "religious fanatic." The answer to this kind of depression is not to become hardened to the evils around us, nor is it to become indifferent to the consequences of sin in society and the eternal destiny of unbelievers. J. B. Phillips has described such a remedy for depression by parodying one of our Lord's beatitudes: "Happy are the hardboiled: for they never let life hurt them."[1] This is the complete opposite of what Jesus said, paradoxical as it may seem: "Blessed are those who mourn, for they shall be comforted" (Mt 5:4). Is there a place, then, for being depressed? Has a Christian any right to be other than depressed in view of the state of the world? When Christian ministers lack the success they naturally want, should they feel depressed? God's treatment of Elijah will help us to answer such questions.

There are also inward causes of depression in the personality. Elijah was the kind of person you expect to get depressed, having strong feelings. If he loved anything, he did so with all his being. The same could be said of his hatreds. Alexander Whyte wrote of him: "There was a great mass of manhood in Elijah. He was a Mount Sinai of a man with a heart like a thunderstorm."[2]

Because he cared about things so deeply, the state of Israel and the mission God gave him demanded of him a heavy price in the realm of his feelings. But God needed a person like that for the decadent days in which he lived. Even though his message was at a complete variance with popular ideas and an unwelcome rebuke to its low standards of morality, he asserted what he believed with uncompromising dogmatism. This was just what the situation demanded. When people are growing careless about spiritual issues, a voice like Elijah's may jerk them out of their complacency. Even if the challenge goes unheeded, it is never wasted, for a faithful and unwavering stand for truth will do much to preserve it for future generations.

At the same time certain weaknesses sometimes accompany the strong points we have described. A zeal for righteousness and truth can go to excess in looking for errors to be denounced, coupled with a moralistic attitude which sees every issue in black and white. Such a person may develop the habit of laying down the law on every controversy in a tone which implies that anyone who thinks otherwise is either deliberately dishonest or just stupid—a characteristic of some politicians! When this style finds its way into the pulpit, it can repel the very people who need a plain statement of the truth. Nor are such foibles confined to the political platform and pulpits. An excessively moralistic outlook and a tyrannical conscience can sour family relationships, when parents impose an impossibly high standard upon their children, turning everything into a moral issue, including genuine accidents. Every lapse is treated as though they did it on purpose, like the duchess in *Alice in Wonderland* who shook her baby violently at the end of each line and sang,

Speak roughly to your little boy,
and beat him when he sneezes;
He only does it to annoy
because he knows it teases.

Further light can be thrown on Elijah by comparing him with his contemporary, Obadiah. He too was devoted to Jehovah, for the Bible informs us that he "was a devout believer" (1 Kings 18:3), and records his own claim that this had been his outlook from his youth (18:12). In personality, however, he was the complete opposite of Elijah. He was a much more thoughtful and sensitive individual. It is difficult to imagine him exercising the outspoken ministry of Elijah, and still harder to visualize him doing what Elijah did on Mount Carmel. Nevertheless Obadiah was especially fitted for the position he held as an employee of Ahab "in charge of his palace" (1 Kings 18:3). It cannot have been easy for a man of God to live in Ahab's household where a variety of gods were worshipped; it called for considerable imagination and tact. One of his achievements was to rescue a hundred prophets of Jehovah from under the very noses of Ahab and Jezebel, hide them in a cave and feed them (18:4).

One cannot imagine Elijah having the delicacy to survive long in such a situation. He would probably have told Ahab and Jezebel in no uncertain terms what he thought of them and gotten himself either thrown out or executed. But God needs the work of an Obadiah as much as an Elijah in the world. A. W. Pink has compared him with other examples in history:

> Where would Luther and the Reformation have been, humanly speaking, had it not been for the Elector of Saxony? And what would have been the fate of Wycliffe if John of Gaunt had not constituted him his ward? As the governor of Ahab's house, Obadiah was undoubtedly in a most difficult and dangerous position, yet so far from bowing his knee to Baal he was instrumental in saving the lives of many of God's servants.[3]

At the same time there are possible weaknesses in Obadiah just as much as in Elijah. The danger for anyone like Obadiah is to compromise and give way on important issues rather than give offense. He has similarities to Timothy, and it seems that Paul detected these same dangers in him when he warned him against giving way to his fears, as we shall discover in a later chapter. Some expositors virtually write off Obadiah for this reason and, although there is no evidence that he ever did compromise, they are noticing a very real danger. Evangelicals today who pride themselves on such diplomacy, should heed such warnings from their brethren.

It is instructive to observe how Elijah and Obadiah each seemed aware of possible shortcomings in one other. Obadiah's view of Elijah is indicated by his reaction to the request to arrange a meeting with Ahab. He protested that the Spirit of God would whisk Elijah away before such a meeting could take place (1 Kings 18:12). He knew that Elijah would readily denounce Ahab from a distance, but he could not imagine him ever meeting him face to face. Subsequent events proved Obadiah wrong, but the point was worth making. It is not unknown today for a preacher to have a great facility for denouncing the failings of the congregation from the pulpit, but find it a very different matter to face them when shaking hands at the church door after the service. This points to a not uncommon deficiency among preachers or, for that matter, any other kind of gifted public speaker. They have great gifts for addressing people in a crowd, but find it difficult to relate to individuals. Is this what Queen Victoria meant when she complained about her prime minister, William Gladstone, "He speaks to me as if I were a public meeting?"

Then what about Elijah's estimation of Obadiah? This may be deduced from his assumption, "I only am left" (19:10 RSV). Of Obadiah and his prophets hiding in the cave he had not a thought. Perhaps he thought that they had all compromised their faith in Jehovah, an assumption which some Christians readily make about each other today. Yet he needed Obadiah when he wanted an introduction to Ahab. Perhaps Elijah had failed to appreciate that, although his own style of ministry was necessary, there is something needed in addition to the public denunciation of error which God was able to provide through Obadiah.

To return to the main theme of this chapter, a person like Elijah can be prone to periods of depression. In his case such a period occurred immediately after he had made a courageous and triumphant stand. When the fire fell from heaven and the prophets of Baal met their fate, all that Elijah stood for and the claims he made, were openly vindicated. The forces of evil had been routed and were in disarray. Yet that was the moment for a man of Elijah's personality to sink into the depths of depression and for the pendulum to swing from triumph to defeat.

Another cause of depression is spiritual and needs to be handled very carefully. To suggest this to depressed Christians can make matters worse. It can add to their sense of guilt which only makes them all the more depressed and sends them into a downward spiral of despair. In any case it is not always clear whether spiritual failure is the cause of depression or its effect. It could equally well be said that the spiritual problems of a depressed person arise through the inability to understand and cope with the depression. Either way, there is a connection between the two as the experience of Elijah clearly demonstrates.

In the first three verses of 1 Kings 19 there is something missing which had been an essential factor in Elijah's ministry right up to the last verse of the previous chapter, "The power of the LORD came upon Elijah" (18:46). There is no mention of that in Elijah's response to Jezebel's murderous threat. What had happened to the courage displayed so recently on Mount Carmel? From what Elijah must have known of Jezebel this development was hardly surprising, but without stopping to lay it before God, he fled from the country. Hitherto he had been sustained by his vision of the living God, but now all he saw was the rage of a murderous woman.

**Four Symptoms of Depression**

The first symptom was his restlessness. Even when he had crossed the frontier into Judah and was out of Jezebel's reach, he did not stop. He left his servant behind at Beersheba and continued a further day's journey into the wilderness until this feverish energy had spent itself, and he lay down exhausted under a broom tree (1 Kings 19:3-4). This common feature of depression can take the form of pacing the floor; or sleeplessness—either the inability to get to sleep, especially if there is anxiety, or waking up early in the morning, if one is dominated by a sense of failure and guilt.

This sense of restlessness has a spiritual dimension in that it robs us of a sense of peace, which God intends for his people. However we feel, we in fact have peace with God, but restlessness means that we are failing to enjoy it. A verse of Eliza Hamilton's describes it well:

This cruel self, O how it strives

And works within my breast,

To come between Thee and my soul

And keep me back from rest.

The next symptom is self-punishment. Elijah expressed it in a suicidal prayer, asking that he might die saying, "I have had enough, LORD. Take my life" (v. 4). This may seem strange for one who had fled from Israel to save his life. But from Elijah's point of view, there was no inconsistency here, for the death he was seeking was not a glorious martyrdom. He had the two most common reasons for suicidal thoughts. One was to see, in death, a way of escape. He felt that he could do no more. He was like the psalmist who longed for "wings like a dove," so that he could "fly away and be at rest" (Ps 55:6). The other reason was blaming himself for failure as he concluded, "I am no better than my ancestors" (v. 4).

A feature of many depressions is directing aggression against oneself, which in extreme cases can lead to suicide. It is not difficult to describe Elijah's depression in these terms. His natural aggression contributed to the strong leadership he displayed on Mount Carmel, when it was directed against the evils of pagan idolatry on Mount Carmel. But this was matched by the intensity with which he then condemned himself for failure to achieve his aims. There is a graphic example of this in the differing reactions of Nehemiah and Ezra. When the former reprimanded some of the Jews for their behavior, he cursed them and "beat some of the men and pulled out their hair" (Neh 13:25). Ezra, on the other hand, faced with a similar situation pulled out his own hair (Ezra 9:3)! Elijah was now behaving like Ezra.

A well-known twentieth-century example of a leader suffering from depression is Winston Churchill, who called it his "black dog." Randolph Churchill's biography of his father reveals how this behavior pattern appeared in his childhood. The young Winston was disapproved of by his father and neglected by his mother, yet he admired them both and blamed himself for their treatment of him. Sir Anthony Storr, in an essay about him, has written, "Psychiatrists have observed that delinquent and emotionally disturbed children, who have parents who are actually neglectful or cruel, still maintain these 'bad' parents are really 'good' and blame themselves for their parents' faults. . . . Winston Churchill showed this idealisation very clearly." Bernard Mobbs adds the following observation, which is full of significance for our present study, "Anthony Storr points out that the one period in Churchill's life when he had little difficulty in coping with his 'black dog' was when, during the second world war, his aggression and hostility could all be directed outward toward the evil tyranny of Hitler's regime."[4]

This could well have been written of Elijah for he, like Churchill during the war, had no problems with depression while he was venting his anger against the religion of Baal. It was in the vacuum that followed that his problem arose with all its intensity, just as it did for Churchill when he was out of office after the war.

Elijah's third symptom is found in his confession of exhaustion. He was referring not to the physical effects of his long journey, but to the emotional fatigue from his efforts against the spiritual state of Israel. He could go no further. He could take no more. Again this is common enough and is the kind of thing that Paul must have had in mind when he urged his readers not to "become weary in doing good" (Gal 6:9). It can, of course, happen to anyone, not least to those engaged in Christian work. It is the weariness that comes to those who, having devoted a great amount of time and effort to a project, fail to see their early hopes realized. This may well be why some Christians lose heart in evangelism. It has been called the "failure syndrome." The memory of past failures saps all enthusiasm from trying again. Elijah, too, was realistic enough to see, that for all the triumphs of Mount Carmel and the nervous energy that he must have expended, the situation in Israel had not changed. So what was there now left for him to do? A minister, who has devoted a great deal of effort for a project, only to be let down by his or her congregation may find him or herself sighing, "It is enough." Hours spent week after week in careful sermon preparation are sometimes difficult to sustain when there is nothing to show for it in the response of the congregation.

At such times it is pertinent to ask what is our motivation. Is our aim little more than the natural human one of wanting to be a success and win the approval of others? Is this the ambition which keeps us going? It is, of course, perfectly natural, but if this is all there is behind our activities, it will not carry us through disappointments. The energy of the flesh can take us so far, but there are obstacles which it cannot surmount.

This leads on logically to Elijah's fourth symptom and especially to the way he describes it. In general it is the feeling of uselessness and failure which is common to all forms of depression. We are naturally dependent on success and tend to feel depressed when we lack it. I wonder how Henry Martyn felt, the missionary pioneer in India, who had only one convert during the whole of his time there. And what about those today who labor in Islamic countries where converts are few and far between? But God does not look at things in the way we so often do. At the end of the Parable of the Talents the master does not compliment his servant on his success, but on his faithfulness. Success depends not only on our ability and diligence, but also on our circumstances. It is no accident that most "successful" ministries in many countries are found in the suburbs among the middle classes. Note how Paul does not rely on success to keep from losing heart. He writes, "Therefore, since through God's mercy we have this ministry, we do not lose heart" (2 Cor 4:1). Whether he sees success or not, he glories in the privilege of being a minister of the Gospel as he described in glowing terms in the previous chapter.

Elijah, however, was haunted by a sense of failure which he expressed by the complaint, "I am no better than my fathers." What did he mean by that? If we take it at its face value, he was admitting that he had wanted to outdo his predecessors and go down in history as the greatest of the prophets. If this is a fair conclusion, it reminds us of the request of the two disciples, "Let one of us sit at your right and the other at your left in your glory" (Mk 10:37).

An insatiable desire to be at the top is the setting for many a frustration and depression today. We can observe it in children (or adults, for that matter) who can enjoy a game only if they win. There are businesspersons who will ruin their health, home, family life and their own character, to satisfy their craving to get to the top, and nothing short of this will do. Those who set themselves the highest goals will suffer the most from frustration. Their tendency will be, as Harold Leavitt in a study of Managerial Psychology has put it, to "feel they are at the bottom unless they are at the top."[5] It is at this point that some seek solace from alcohol which can make them at least feel on top.

This desire to be at the top can sadly intrude into Christian work and complicate relationships. It has not been unknown for Christians of eminence to be reluctant to take part in an enterprise unless they are in the lead. Among lesser persons it has often been a cause of disunity when, for example, a break-away group has formed under a leader who prefers to be a big fish in a little pond than to be scarcely noticed in a larger one. We need to be aware of the possibility that some who aspire to leadership in their church are simply compensating for failure to be at the top in their daily work.

True greatness in God's kingdom is the complete opposite of how the world views it. Some may say that Elijah's problem was that he needed to learn to love himself so that he could love God and others. Yet, self-love is not something that fallen humanity needs any help with. According to A. W. Tozer, "Self-derogation is bad for the reason that self must be there to derogate. Self, whether swaggering or grovelling, can never be anything but hateful to God. . . . Boasting is an evidence that we are pleased with self; belittling, that we are disappointed in it. Either way we reveal that we have a high opinion of ourselves."[6] It is the way of the One who said, "Whoever wants to be first must be slave of all. For even the Son of Man did not come to be served, but to serve, and to give his life as a ransom for many" (Mk 10:44-45). Other well-known words of Jesus, which have something to say to those who are suffering from the frustrations we are considering, are "But many who are first will be last, and many who are last will be first" (Mt 19:30). Elijah, even though he wrote himself off as a failure, has indeed been attested by history as one of the greatest of the prophets.

**Initial Treatment**

How did God deal with his depressed servant? We begin with two negatives. First God did not forsake him. Depression often includes the feeling that God has turned away and become distant. Although Elijah did not make this complaint, we find it in the Psalms. Take for example Psalm 77, in which the sufferers reveal the thoughts which had bothered them as they lay awake at night:

"Will the Lord reject forever?
Will he never show his favor again?
Has his unfailing love vanished forever?
Has his promise failed for all time?
Has God forgotten to be merciful?
Has he in anger withheld his compassion?" (Ps 77:7-9)

The psalmist seems to recognize that these questionings have nothing to do with the real facts about God, but simply reflect his own condition. This is brought out by the older version of verse 10, which Derek Kidner prefers,[7] "And I said, This *is* my infirmity" (Ps 77:10 KJV). The doubts he has thrown upon God simply result from the sickness in his mind and say nothing of the truth about God and his faithfulness. As the Psalmist affirms in the following verses, this has been proven in the past and is not affected by his changing feelings. Elijah too had proven

God's faithfulness on Mount Carmel and immediately afterwards "the power of the LORD came upon Elijah" (1 Kings 18:46). Nothing which had since gone on in Elijah's mind could change that. As Paul once reassured his young colleague, "if we are faithless, he will remain faithful, for he cannot disown himself" (2 Tim 2:13).

There is also an absence of any condemnation of Elijah. That does not mean that God condoned his state of mind. But there was no need to condemn Elijah for the simple reason that he was condemning himself already, and there was no need to add to it. Also God understands our weaknesses as the Psalmist recognized:

"As a father has compassion on his children,

so the LORD has compassion on those who fear him;

For he knows how we are formed,

he remembers that we are dust." (Ps 103:13-14)

Our weaknesses arise largely out of the limitations of our physical nature. Everyone knows this from experience. We are more likely to be irritable when we are physically tired and impatient when we are hungry. During times of illness, it may be difficult for us to view our lives in their right perspective.

Here was a factor that governed the initial treatment which God prescribed for Elijah. Before probing his spiritual problems, he was given food and sleep. Prolonged sleep is a common therapy for those suffering from stress, which is what the angel provided for Elijah, waking him for food and then allowing him further sleep (1 Kings 19:5-7). When coping with the strains of spiritual leadership, we do well to observe the common-sense rules of physical health. After God had attended to these needs, Elijah arose a different man. "Strengthened by that food, he traveled forty days and forty nights until he reached Horeb, the mountain of God" (v. 8). No longer was he running away from Jezebel. Instead he had the positive aim of meeting God on the mountain where he had revealed himself to Moses centuries earlier.

**The Problem Exposed**

It was in the cave on Mount Sinai that God dealt with the spiritual issues which were involved in Elijah's depression and showed him how to regard the discouraging situation in apostate Israel. Twice he asked him, "What are you doing here, Elijah?" and twice Elijah had to put into words what was on his heart. Here is an important step in coping with any problem—to understand clearly what is bothering us by putting it into words. Elijah spelled out the spiritual concerns which lay on his heart. These were no doubt intensified by Mount Sinai, which was associated with all that Elijah held dear. It was here that God had first made himself known to Moses at the burning bush, and later he had given him the law which the Israelites were now treating so lightly. Here, surely, Elijah had every reason to be deeply concerned, just as we should be today when contemplating the spiritual state of the world in which we live. Indeed, how can we preach with reality unless we care and, like Elijah, are jealous for the Lord? Does this mean then, that we ought to conduct our ministry for God in a state of depression? That depends partly on whether Elijah was correct in his next complaint, "I am the only one left, and now they are trying to kill me too" (19:14).

If it were true that he was the sole surviving adherent of Jehovah, and that once he was dead the worship of Jehovah would die out altogether, the situation would indeed have been hopeless. It would have meant that Elijah represented the last futile attempt to reverse the trend. But, this is where he had things out of proportion. He should have known perfectly well that he was not the only one left. He had met Obadiah and had heard from his lips about the hundred prophets hidden in the cave. But a man of Elijah's temperament is, as we have already seen, all too ready to write off people like Obadiah and his friends. They begin to feel that they are the only faithful ones left, and the only hope for the church will die with them. In some cases one can even detect a morbid kind of satisfaction in being prophets of gloom and doom. So how does God show that, although the spiritual state of Israel should be the cause of deep concern, it does not demand the depressive reaction to which Elijah had succumbed? We now come to the heart of the matter, as we consider how God dealt with Elijah in the cave on Mount Sinai.

## A Still Small Voice

The answer to Elijah's problem was given in a somewhat unexpected form. He was first given an impressive display of God's power—a wind which was so strong that it broke rocks, an earthquake and a fire. Now although these phenomena would normally have been regarded as manifestations of the presence of God, on this particular occasion "the LORD was not in the wind. . . . the LORD was not in the earthquake. . . . the LORD was not in the fire" (1 Kings 19:11-12). It was not until the noise of these had faded away that God finally spoke, and then, in complete contrast to all that had just occurred, it was in "a gentle whisper."

An obvious explanation advanced by some interpreters, is that Elijah had to learn not to depend on the miraculous and sensational. After Mount Carmel and the dramatic events in which he had been involved there, he needed to appreciate that God also works in quieter ways through, for example, a personality like that of Obadiah. There is, of course, undoubted truth in this. The people of our Lord's day, with their requests for signs from heaven to vindicate his claims, could have profited from this lesson. It is what is said of the Holy Spirit in a Pentecost hymn:

And his that gentle voice we hear
Soft as the breath of even.

At the same time there seems to be a deeper significance in the manner in which God spoke to Elijah with particular relevance to his condition. We have to remember that the wind, earthquake and fire were reminiscient of the manifestations which had accompanied the giving of the law through Moses (Ex 19:16-19). They spoke to Elijah of essential truths about the holiness of God, which were at the center of all that Elijah stood for, and which Israel had sadly forgotten. When the law had first been given, the Israelites had trembled at the manifestation of God's presence. If only they could be made to do that now!

We are now looking at a factor which can play a large part in the depression of Christians who tend to be excessively moralistic. They are deeply aware of God's law and set themselves high standards, seeing moral issues in black and white but, human as they are, they never achieve them and so are always undermined by a sense of failure. When they try to impose those standards on others, again, they are up against human frailty. It can produce a sad state of affairs in a family in which extremely strict parents wage a constant battle with the shortcomings of their children. The same can be said when it dominates the pulpit; the more sensitive members of the congregation are in a state of continual self-condemnation as they are repeatedly reminded of their failures.

Is what we have described, then, a wrong conception of God? By no means, because this was how God had revealed himself when giving his law. He certainly makes moral demands which none of us has succeeded in satisfying. Moreover, a healthy fear of God is what many people sadly lack today, no less than in Elijah's time. How then did Elijah need to be put right? What he and those like him need to learn is that this is not the whole truth about God. It is not that God is never in the wind, earthquake and fire. At times he certainly is. But what Elijah needed was to be assured that God is also full of grace to those who love him, and even in wrath he would remember mercy. If a God of grace did not condemn Elijah, why need he condemn himself? God could well have addressed Elijah in New Testament language: "You have not come to a mountain that can be touched and that is burning with fire; to darkness, gloom and storm; to a trumpet blast or to such a voice speaking words that those who heard it begged that no further word be spoken to them. . . . But you have come to Mount Zion." (Heb 12:18-22).

One does sometimes encounter extreme pathological cases of depressed Christians who find it difficult to grasp the free grace of God. They give lip service to the unmerited grace of God and his complete forgiveness, but still find a way to blame themselves. If their justification is received simply by faith, then they imagine that somehow the strength of their faith contribute to their acceptance by God, and they blame themselves because their faith is not sufficient. Or they can dwell on sins and failures and, instead of resting in the assurance that through the death of Christ, they are completely forgiven, they still persist in punishing themselves for them. They find Bible texts to use as sticks to beat themselves with, even though it involves applying to themselves passages which have nothing to do with those whose sins are covered by the blood of Christ. Paul Tournier describes how

　　instead of drawing from the Bible the marvellous consolation which is there precisely for them, they have a morbid passion for hunting out texts on the severity of God, His wrath, curses and punishments. They torment themselves in this way with Bible references not directed at them, and increase their distress by the implacable condemnations which do not concern them at all.[8]

One such Bible reference they may well latch onto sooner or later is the so-called unpardonable sin (Mk 3:29), convincing themselves that they have committed it and are therefore numbered among those whom it is impossible to restore again to repentence (Heb 6:4-6).

Some depressed Christians seem to be suffering from what Paul calls "the spirit of slavery" (Rom 8:15 RSV). Dr. Martyn Lloyd-Jones selected this as an example of spiritual depression in his collection of studies on this subject. He observed that "the slave attitude generally arises from the tendency to turn the Christian life into a new law, into a higher law."[9] The way of the Holy Spirit is quite different: "But you did not receive the spirit of slavery to fall back into fear, but you have received the spirit of sonship. When we cry, '*Abba*, Father!' it is the Spirit himself bearing witness with our spirit that we are children of God" (Rom 8:15-16 RSV). The realization of this truth removes the spirit of bondage. How does it do it? Here is how Dr. Lloyd-Jones explains it:

It enables us to see that our object in living the Christian Life is not simply to attain a certain standard, but is rather to please God because he is our Father—"the spirit of adoption whereby we cry, Abba, Father." The slave was not allowed to say "Abba" and that slave spirit does not regard God as Father. He has not realized that He is Father, he regards Him still as a Judge who condemns. But that is wrong. As Christian people we must learn to appropriate by faith the fact that

God is our Father. That is our relationship to God and the moment we realize it, it transforms everything.[10]

This does not mean that we lose our fear of God. But it is not a craven fear. In response to the quiet voice Elijah "pulled his cloak over his face" (1 Kings 19:13), for the God of grace and mercy commands our reverence every bit as much as the God of wrath.

There now remains the tragedy of Israel's apostasy which confronted Elijah, and the state of a fallen world with which we are surrounded today. Even though we may learn not to punish ourselves for our failures, have we any right to be other than depressed over the state of the world if we are jealous for the Lord? It is this question which is answered by what the quiet voice says to Elijah.

## God's Answer

First, God instructed Elijah to anoint Hazael to the Syrian throne and Jehu over Israel. This may come as a surprise to us as it probably was to Elijah. None of the previous kings of the northern kingdom of Israel had been anointed by a prophet, and to anoint a king for the heathen Syrian nation is even more questionable. Furthermore neither proved to be particularly attractive candidates for their positions. Hazael obtained his throne by murdering his predecessor (2 Kings 8:15), while Jehu did the same and then exterminated the entire royal family. Of this, God expressed his disapproval when he revealed to Hosea, "I will soon punish the house of Jehu for the massacre at Jezreel" (Hos 1:4). The Bible's verdict on his reign is that he "was not careful to keep the law of the LORD, the God of Israel, with all his heart. He did not turn away from the sins of Jeroboam, which he had caused Israel to commit" (2 Kings 10:31). It is true that he did not worship Baal, but he continued the idolatry of the high places and the degrading practices that went with it.

Why then was the prophet of the Lord told to anoint these godless kings? Was it not to demonstrate that, in spite of their apparent power and the way in which they obtained their thrones, God is sovereign over them and it is by him that kings reign (Prov 8:15)? They rule only by divine permission and God sets them up and brings them down as he pleases, overruling them to fulfil his purposes. Thus he chose to use Hazael and Jehu to exterminate the worship of Baal (1 Kings 19:17), just as later he delivered his people from exile by the intervention of the heathen king Cyrus. For Christian people today who feel depressed about the state of the world and the apparent power of its anti-Christian rulers, this is worth remembering. The most powerful dictator is allowed to continue only as long as God decrees. The truth is the basis for one of the prayers for the sovereign in the Book of Common Prayer: "We are taught by thy holy Word, that the hearts of kings are in thy rule and governance, and that thou dost dispose and turn them as it seemeth best to thy godly wisdom."

Elijah is next commissioned to anoint his successor, Elisha (1 Kings 19:16, 19-21). Here, again, was just the answer to one of his worries. Not only would he have the companionship of a younger man, but also the assurance that God had made adequate provision for the future. When Elijah's ministry ultimately came to an end, the witness to Jehovah would continue. Like many outstanding and aging leaders since, who have been tempted to think of themselves and their generation as the final hope for the future, he had to learn that God was about to use a younger man with a personality very different from his own. It was also evidence that God in his grace, mercy and patience, would still give Israel the spiritual opportunities of a prophet's ministry.

God then added a further corrective for those filled with pessimism about the prospects for God's kingdom. Elijah had made the depressing assumption that he was the only one in Israel still true to Jehovah, to which God replied, with the assurance, "Yet I reserve seven thousand in Israel—all whose knees have not bowed to Baal and all whose mouths have not kissed him" (1 Kings 19:18).

This is the reassuring doctrine of the remnant, that even in the darkest days, when everyone seems to have turned away from God, he preserves a remnant of those who remain faithful. Without it there were times in Old Testament history when the outlook would have been bleak indeed, as Isaiah recognized when faced with a similar situation in the southern kingdom of Judah: "Except the LORD of hosts had left unto us a very small remnant, we should have been as Sodom, and we should have been like unto Gomorrah" (Isa 1:9, KJV).

The situation was similar at the dawn of the New Testament era. The visible church had fallen into many errors during the intertestamental period, and contemporary Judaism was a heresy and not the religion of the Old Testament. It comes as no surprise that when the promised Messiah appeared, they failed to recognize him. Nevertheless, there was a faithful remnant including those like Mary, Joseph, Simeon and Anna, who were "waiting for the consolation of Israel" and for the "redemption of Jerusalem" (Lk 2:25, 38). It was such as these who welcomed Jesus as the Messiah and, although the exact nature of his mission they did not yet appreciate, they were able to recognize him even when he was only a helpless babe. Throughout subsequent history, it has been the same. In days when the cause of the Gospel has seemed lost in apostasy and unbelief, God in his grace and mercy has preserved a remnant of true believers.

Moreover Elijah may well have been further surprised by the

size of the remnant in his day. Even if he had given grudging recognition to Obadiah and his hundred prophets hiding in the cave, that was still a long way short of the seven thousand who had remained true. John made the same discovery, but on a far greater scale. In the forced labor camp on the isle of Patmos, when the tiny Christian minority seemed so powerless compared with the might of imperial Rome, it must have been far from easy to be optimistic about the prospects for the Gospel. Yet, when given a glimpse behind the scenes into heaven, he was given a vision of the ultimate triumph of Christ—the Lamb upon the throne—and the number of God's redeemed people. They were not an insignificant handful but "a great multitude that no one could count" (Rev 7:9).

When we look out upon a fallen world and the state of the professing church, like Elijah we can find much cause for depression. But what we see around us is only part of the truth. We need to take into account the sovereignty of God, his authority over the powers of this world and his provision for the future. There is also the believing remnant which he always preserves, and this is much larger than we imagine in our more pessimistic moments. Here is one of the ways that those who care enough to mourn will be comforted (Mt 5:4).

Imperial Rome, like the throne of Ahab and Jezebel to Elijah, must have seemed overwhelmingly powerful to the persecuted Christians of the early centuries. They must sometimes have wondered how the church could survive against such odds. But it was Rome, like many empires since, which eventually crumbled while the church has been preserved.

Crowns and thrones may perish,
Kingdoms rise and wane,
But the Church of Jesus
Constant will remain;

Gates of Hell can never
'Gainst that Church prevail;
We have Christ's own promise,
And that cannot fail.

## Questions for Groups and Individuals

1. Do you know any spiritual leaders who suffer from depression. Describe them.

2. What do you think are the causes of depression today? (pp. 61-62)

3. Describe the differences between Obadiah and Elijah. (pp. 63-65) Describe Obadiahs and Elijahs you have seen in leadership.

4. What are the four symptoms of depression? (pp. 66-70) When have you seen these forces at work in your friends and acquaintances?

5. How can society's values lead to depression? (pp. 70-71)

6. How did God care for Elijah? (pp. 71-73) What does this show you about how you can relate to depressed persons?

7. Why do you think God chose to speak to Elijah in a whisper? (pp. 75-77) How can you apply this in your ministry?

8. How can an inadequate conception of God lead to depression? (pp. 76-79)

9. The author mentions three actions God took which helped to alleviate Elijah's depression. (pp. 79-81) How did each of these things meet Elijah's needs?

10. How has God encouraged you in times of need?

# 5

# IN THE SHADOW OF A MENTOR

## Elisha

ELISHA SHOWS US HOW TO DEAL WITH TWO DIFFICULTIES WHICH many have to face. Both arise from the stature of Elijah. On the one hand he was Elisha's predecessor and was likely to cast a very big shadow over his ministry. He was also the mentor Elisha depended on. But Elisha would have to take on the great responsibilities ahead without having Elijah to lean upon.

It seems that Elisha himself was aware of this in the way that he related his own ministry to Elijah. He asked for "a double portion" of Elijah's spirit because he respected Elijah so much (2 Kings 2:9). When he had to recross the Jordan just after Elijah was taken, he used his mantle in the way that his master had done, calling, "Where now is the LORD, the God of Elijah?" (2:14). But Elijah was gone, and Elisha was on his own like a pilot flying solo for the first time. Perhaps the way that he insisted on staying with Elijah right to the end of his last journey (2 Kings 2:2, 4, 6) indicates that he did not relish the thought of being left to carry on his ministry without him. Also, he did not take too kindly to the sons of the prophets airing their knowledge about Elijah's forthcoming departure and asked them to be quiet (2 Kings 2:3, 5).

Elisha's experience was one which I can relate too. I served my first four years in two pastorates under the direction of two older clergymen who helped me considerably. After that, at a young age, I was given sole charge in a challenging situation in the center of London. Then, I had to take full responsibility for my decisions. The mistakes I had made in my first two churches I had left conveniently behind, but from now on my mistakes would be my own. I would have to pick up myself and live with the consequences, perhaps, for a number of years. The transition was not too easy, and it was then that I discovered how lonely the Christian ministry can be. I strongly suspect that Elisha found the same, only in his case it was much worse. He faced a far tougher situation than most of us have to cope with, and he couldn't reach Elijah at the other end of a telephone line!

There was also another difficulty in taking over from Elijah—he was Elisha's predecessor. What a man to have to follow! Elijah would long be remembered as the one who had defied the prophets of Baal on Mount Carmel and whose prayers had been answered by fire from heaven. Elisha had no doubt about how those who cherished the cause of Jehovah would miss him. As Elijah was taken from him he exclaimed, "My father, my father! The chariots and the horsemen of Israel!" (2:12). Presumably, he meant that Elijah was worth more to Israel than all its horses and chariots.

The sons of the prophets also seemed to long for Elijah's return since, in spite of their awareness that Elijah was to be taken from them, they insisted on searching for him (2 Kings 2:15-18). This is always the way with an outstanding ministry, and accounts for the difficulty a successor has in following it. And it can happen at every level of ministry.

I knew of a young pastor who confessed to his bishop his difficulty in following his highly successful predecessor. The bishop replied that during his own first few years he felt the shadow of his predecessor everywhere in the community.

Church members may contribute to this problem, and it is not always the immediate predecessor that they bring up. In one of my churches, I inherited a very run-down situation and was beginning to see some growth. Yet, one of the elderly members was far from satisfied and frustrated me by repeatedly telling me of the good old days with a very distinguished ministry when the church was filled to capacity.

How then did Elisha approach the daunting prospect of succeeding Elijah and assuming his responsibilities without the benefit of Elijah's support? The two utterances which we quoted at the beginning of the chapter point to the answer to this question. The first was addressed to Elijah in response to the invitation, "Tell me, what can I do for you?": "Let me inherit a double portion of your spirit" (2 Kings 2:9). The second was his call after Elijah had left him: "Where now is the LORD, the God of Elijah?" (2 Kings 2:14).

### Let Me Inherit a Double Portion of Your Spirit

What did Elisha mean by a "double portion of Elijah's spirit"? Did he want to have twice the gifts that Elijah possessed? Elijah might well have wished it for his successor, but it seems hardly likely that Elisha would have asked for something so offensive to Elijah just before his departure.

The explanation is that Elisha was using the language of inheritance and simply asking for the portion due to the first-born. His desire was to be a worthy successor of Elijah and to maintain his standard of ministry. He wanted to live up to the expectations which were implied when Elijah's mantle had first fallen upon his shoulders. He was not asking to be a replica of Elijah, nor was he going to imitate his methods. He simply wanted to inherit the inward spirituality which empowered his ministry. By making this request, he was humbly recognizing his need, and looking to God to equip him with the gifts necessary to fulfill what was to be demanded of him.

After Elijah's departure, there was soon evidence that his request had been granted. When confronted with the Jordan, he did what Elijah had done, acting on the assumption that God had answered his prayer. The waters were parted and the sons of the prophets made the observation, "the spirit of Elijah is resting on Elisha" (2 Kings 2:13-15). We may not expect the same sort of miracle today, but the principle holds good—God always supplies the gifts appropriate to our calling, and we prove our ministry by exercising them. "Do not neglect your gift" (1 Tim 4:14) was Paul's advice to his young disciple and successor.

### Where Now Is the LORD, the God of Elijah?

There are three observations I wish to make of this call from the lips of Elisha. First, it shows that he shared Elijah's undivided consecration to Jehovah and the purity of life associated with his worship, which contrasted sharply to the rival religions making their claims on Israel. Without such an agreement Elisha would have benefited little from his association with Elijah and would have been ill-prepared for what lay ahead. This

principle is no less true today. There are certain basic theological priorities on which there must be agreement for effective
working relationships.

The accord between Elijah and Elisha was apparent from the
moment he first found him hard at work with a plow in one
of his father's fields. When Elijah threw his cloak over him,
sudden though it was, he knew what it meant and was ready for
it. He responded by running after Elijah with the promise that
he would follow him as soon as he had said good-bye to his
parents. Even though Elisha could have expected to inherit the
wealth of his prosperous father, once he was called to be first
Elijah's disciple and then his successor, he put all that behind
him.

And, as if to make it impossible for himself ever to turn back
from following Elijah, Elisha made a fire of the wood of his
familiar plough, and slew his favorite oxen and made a feast
of the flesh, and thereby proclaimed openly to all men that
he had put his hand to another plough than that plough of
wood, from which he would never draw back. Elisha burned
his ships that day, as the Romans would have said.[1]
We would say today that he had burned his bridges behind him.
His devotion to Jehovah and the lifestyle that went with it was
still clear for all to see years later as exemplified by the observation that "this man who often comes our way is a holy man
of God" (2 Kings 4:9).

The second observation on Elisha's call for "the God of Elijah" is that it reveals an important point in his favor as he took
over leadership—he had been a good disciple. This showed
itself immediately after Elijah had been taken from him. On his
return journey he had to recross the river Jordan, but this time
without Elijah. So he struck the water with the cloak as he had
seen Elijah do and then called, not for Elijah, nor for God, but

for "the God of Elijah." By this Elisha was openly acknowledging that much of what he knew about God, he had learned from Elijah. This demonstrates what a good disciple he had been, that he had been loyal to Elijah, willing to depend on him and learn from him. Elisha was later described as one who "used to pour water on the hands of Elijah" (2 Kings 3:11).

Being willing to serve under older colleagues and learn from them, even if we feel that in many respects we know better, is a mark of maturity. The way we conduct ourselves at that stage can be an indication of whether we can be entrusted with a sole charge of our own. The apostles of the New Testament were first called *disciples*, while the supreme example is our Lord himself in the Temple at the age of twelve. The world too has its examples of persons who have risen to great heights, who, in their younger days, were eager to learn from their elders.

Winston Churchill was one who did this. His son, Randolph, has written of his father's earlier years: "Churchill took advantage of his father's family connections . . . to make the acquaintance of many of Lord Randolph's (Winston's father) friends and associates."[2] Winston, wrote to his mother in 1896 about the interesting people he had met at a party, such as Asquith, Balfour and Lord Rothschild: "I appreciate meeting such clever people and listening to their conversation very much indeed."[3]

Old Testament history records the tragic example of one who did the opposite—Rehoboam. He ignored the advice of older men and listened instead to his peers, who flattered him and told him what he wanted to hear. The result was disastrous and led to him losing his leadership over a large part of the nation. Assistants in ministry today, who feel tempted to disloyalty, can often find dissidents who will flatter them and encourage them to go their own way. If they allow this to happen, it will invariably spoil their future ministry. Indeed, it may well lead to their disqualification for the ministry altogether.

I remember it being instilled into me at Bible college: Be loyal to your elders in Christian ministry, even when you disagree with them and, above all, don't allow yourself to become head of the opposition party! (This is a management principle which is widely acknowledged in secular society as well.) I also recall being told that I was to learn from my superiors and not to attempt to train them.

This was brought home to me during my first pastorate when a visiting preacher pointed to some of the things I could learn from my senior pastor (whom he himself had known personally for many years). The congregation where I served my second pastorate included an elderly retired clergyman who had a long and distinguished ministry. I often accepted his invitation to drop in for a cup of coffee so that I could listen to his reminiscences. Because of his age, I sometimes heard the same story more than once, but this mattered little because I learned so much from him. Then when I had my first assistant, the roles were reversed. He was a little older than me, and I had been ordained only six and a half years when he joined me. But it soon became apparent that he intended to extract all he could of my experience those six and a half years—little though it may have been.

The third observation is that although Elisha was united to Elijah by a common devotion to Jehovah, and although he looked up to him, there were, at the same time marked differences in their personalities. For one thing Elisha was a gentler and more sensitive person. Also Elijah had left behind him a reputation for standing up to ungodly and antagonistic people, including Ahab and Jezebel, in a way that one cannot imagine Elisha doing. I cannot, for example, visualize him in Elijah's shoes on Mount Carmel.

Such differences in temperament must always be taken into account, as they affect our leadership style. We should never expect a junior colleague to operate in exactly the same way we would, nor must we try to press them into the same mold. The younger persons, for their parts, should pause before criticizing seniors for their methods, which may well result from their personality and differing gifts. In Christian service it is essential that we be ourselves. All of us have to work out the right way for us to go about God's work, using the gifts we have been given.

Again I recall my first experience of having an assistant minister. Many observed how different we were, thus complementing each other in a very constructive way. I was quite sure that my colleague, had he been the senior pastor, would have done many things differently from me, as indeed he has during his subsequent ministry. So it was with Elijah and Elisha, who were very different from each other.

To begin with, however, it was natural for Elisha to model himself after the one he admired, just as many of us do today, even to the extent of copying their mannerisms. Elisha started out on his public life in Elijah's coat of camel's hair and his leather girdle. But this did not really suit Elisha's more casual style, so he soon discarded them and was content to be himself. He was like the Philippians in the absence of Paul, who had to work out their "salvation with fear and trembling." He had the assurance that God was working in him (as did the Philippians, Phil 2:12-13) as much as he had been in Elijah.

This needs to be born in mind when comparing church leaders with their predecessors. I recently heard an elderly gentleman speaking of the many ministers he had seen come and go during his long church membership. "They were all different," he explained. And no doubt that was all part of the econ-

omy of God. It is not difficult to see how changing circumstances in Israel called for a different style of prophetic ministry. During the reign of Ahab, the threat from the religion of
Baal called for an Elijah to stand against it. With the accession
of Jehoram the situation changed somewhat. Although the new
king "clung to the sins of Jeroboam son of Nebat, which he had
caused Israel to commit," he "got rid of the sacred stone of Baal
that his father had made" (2 Kings 3:2-3). Alexander Whyte
draws the following lesson from it: "No men among us need
more to be men of today, and not of yesterday, than they who
preach the Word of God to us and to our children. Even the
Elijah you so often go back upon, were he here again, he would
not be exactly the same man, with exactly the same mantle."[4]

This surely has much to say to us. As we are weaned from
those who have taken responsibility for us, and as we take over
leadership when others have laid it down, we need to remember that all of us are empowered by the same Spirit, just
as Elijah and Elisha were. All of us owe a loyalty to the same
basic truths and priorities. All of us must be willing to learn,
sometimes from those who are very different from us in style
and personality. But we must be ourselves, the people God
wants us to be and using the gifts which he has seen fit to give
to us for the situation to which he has called us.

### Questions for Individuals or Groups

1. Describe a mentor you have had. What was your relationship like?

2. If you have been separated from that person, describe your feelings
when it occured.

3. Describe what you've seen happen when someone follows a very successful predecessor. (pp. 85-86)

4. Who's spirit would you request a double portion of if you had an opportunity like Elisha's? (pp. 87-88) Why?

5. What do you think an attitude of willingness to learn about older Christian leaders reveals? (pp. 89-91)

6. Why is it important that senior leaders allow for juniors to develop their ministries in ways that may differ from their own? (pp. 91-93)

7. When has it been difficult for you to learn from a supervisor? How did you resolve the situation?

# 6
# MARITAL STRESS
## Hosea

F EW PEOPLE, READING ABOUT THE CALL OF HOSEA FOR THE FIRST time, could fail to be shocked by the blunt statement: "When the LORD began to speak through Hosea, the LORD said to him, 'Go, take to yourself an adulterous wife and children of unfaithfulness' " (Hos 1:2). What a start for the ministry of a prophet. He is told to marry a prostitute! What follows is no surprise: a disastrous marriage. His wife bore three children and, of at least one of them, Hosea was not the father. Just think what this meant for Hosea, exercising a ministry for God and, presumably trying to live a life in keeping with it.

All around him was a corrupt society with low moral standards, especially in relationships between men and women. Much of the immoral behavior went on in the name of the idolatrous religion they followed, being encouraged by temple prostitutes who were part of it. Maintaining standards and ministering in such circumstances is difficult enough. But then Hosea had an added problem—his own marriage was broken down by his wife sleeping around with other men! How could he continue to make a stand on these issues when his own house needed to be put in order? We naturally wonder how many fingers were pointed at him, but the biblical narrative leaves that to our imagination.

This is not unlike what we sometimes find today. We too live in the midst of a morally corrupt society and have to contend with the many social ills that result. Marriages have been breaking down on a large scale and depressing statistics are often produced. Church members are by no means immune, and local pastors find that marriage counselling makes considerable demands on their time. And then, what seems to be worst of all, their own marriages come under strain. We are not suggesting that there are many cases as extreme as Hosea's, but what some Christian leaders experience today is not dissimilar.

Another area of difficulty is in bringing up children. With the pressures upon young people today it is not an easy matter to bring up children in the faith and to ensure that they observe Christian moral standards especially in sexual behavior. Family relationships can undergo considerable strain as children pass through their teen-age years, and pastors are often called upon to console brokenhearted Christian parents. Then, having handed out advice to other parents they become aware that one or more of their own children are turning away from the Lord.

Experiences like this can burden Christian leaders' hearts with guilt and a sense of shame and undermine their ministries. As they stand in front of an audience or congregation, the devil is adept at whispering reminders which seem to disqualify them from ministering to others. I heard only recently of a Christian leader who had been so shattered when his teen-age daughter became pregnant that he gave up full-time Christian work and took a secular job.

How do we cope with this kind of thing or support our fellow ministers if it happens to them? The experience of Hosea has much to teach us.

## He Saw It as Under the Sovereignty of God

Commentators have raised various questions about Hosea's marriage. Was his wife already living an immoral life when he married her, or did she turn to it later? Did Hosea know at the time of their marriage the kind of woman she was or would turn out to be? Of one thing, however, the Bible leaves us in no doubt—Hosea, far from blaming himself for his choice of a marriage partner or for what subsequently happened to his relationship with her, saw it as being under the sovereignty of God. That is not to say that Hosea bore no blame for what happened. He was a sinner like the rest of us, so we would not be surprised if he handled the situation imperfectly and to that extent made it worse. The important point to grasp is that Hosea's unhappy marriage was God's will for him and, because he was led into it when the "LORD began to speak" through him (Hos 1:2), it was closely related to the ministry to which God called him.

This surely is how we must always regard the strains and stresses that come upon us. They may result immediately from the sins of others or even from our own, and we should treat them accordingly, seeking God's forgiveness. But we should also recognize that in some way beyond our comprehension, they are brought about by the sovereign purpose of God.

There are other examples in Scripture, such as Joseph, whom

we have already considered. He was handed over to slavery through the sins of his brothers, of which they later repented. Yet, as we have seen and as Joseph later assured his brothers, he saw it as God's way of bringing him to Egypt. The supreme example is the death of Christ. It was the foulest deed of sinful humanity in the whole of history to put cruelly to death the spotless Son of God, yet, as Isaiah put it, "It was the Lord's will to crush him" (Is 53:10). Peter made the same point on the Day of Pentecost. "This man was handed over to you by God's set purpose and foreknowledge" (Acts 2:23).

At the same time he did not exonerate the Jerusalem leaders, but described them as "lawless men." Nor did Judas escape from blame, because even though, as Jesus said, "The Son of Man will go just as it is written about him," he added: "But woe to that man who betrays the Son of Man! It would be better for him if he had not been born" (Mt 26:24).

The question then to be faced is why does God allow this kind of thing to happen? It is surely to mold us for the particular ministry he has for us. Any Christian undergoing difficult times ought to ask, "How can I turn this to God's glory? What is God teaching me through this?" And a leader ought to add the further question, "How can this deepen my ministry for God?"

It is made very clear that in Hosea's case the trials into which God had led him were closely linked to the challenge he faced and the kind of ministry it demanded. Note the reason God gave for the marriage he had chosen for Hosea: "because the land is guilty of the vilest adultery in departing from the LORD" (Hos 1:2). The Old Testament sees the relationship between God and his people as a marriage, Israel's apostasy as a broken covenant and following other gods as adultery. Hosea's marriage experience, then, was not unlike what was happening to Israel.

This must be why God sometimes allows Christian leaders to carry burdens, including family worries. The people who are our nearest and dearest can hurt us most, and this applies no less to God himself. So here is a way of deepening our understanding of how God feels when we turn away from him and go our own way.

I knew of a minister who had an unpleasant scene with one of his teen-age children on a Saturday evening (such things always seem to happen in families on Saturdays!). Like many Christian parents he found it difficult to reprimand his children without feeling guilty afterward especially when, as in this case, it involved an argument. The next day was, of course, Sunday, and with memories of the night before still fresh in his mind, he had to drag himself into the pulpit to preach a sermon for which he felt woefully inadequate. To his amazement somebody afterwards thanked him for the special help received, adding, "You preached with extra sensitivity this morning!"

## Mercy and Judgment

Hosea had to preach during one of the darkest periods of Israel's history. The attempt to compromise the religion of Jehovah with idolatrous Canaanite ritual and associated immoral practices of the most degrading kind was having a disastrous effect on the nation. Everywhere were the marks of decay with declining moral standards. How should one respond to such a situation? There are two alternatives.

One is righteous indignation. This calls for severe laws, a strong police force to enforce them and severe penalties for offenders. The church would stress eternal punishment with hellfire preachers to proclaim it. The other alternative is the soft approach. The approach is to show understanding and love, appeal to people's better feelings. God is represented as

taking a tolerant view of human sin like a benevolent grand-
father who says "boys will be boys." Offenders are not wicked
and deserving punishment, but sick and needing pity.

As is so often the case with contradictory approaches, both
attitudes contain truth, and the Bible certainly includes both.
God declares his wrath against sinners and hell is a reality
demanded by his righteousness. "It is a dreadful thing to fall
into the hands of the living God" (Heb 10:31). At the same time
he is the God of infinite love "who desireth not the death of
a sinner" (Book of Common Prayer). Coexisting with the wrath
which burns against our sins is the heart of a Father who understands our weaknesses: "As a father has compassion on his
children, so the LORD has compassion on those who fear him;
for he knows how we are formed; he remembers that we are
dust" (Ps 103:13-14). Nowhere is the balance between these two
sides of the character of God more clearly maintained than in
Hosea. A key verse to his main theme is, "I will betroth you in
righteousness and justice, in love and compassion" (Hos 2:19).

"Righteousness and justice" speak of the forbidding standards of a holy God, while "love and compassion" declare his
love for the sinner who deserves his judgment. Hosea was like
the Psalmist who sang "of mercy and judgement" (Ps 101:1
KJV).

### Hosea's Message
Chapter 4 provides an example of God's indictment against
Israel described in verse 1 as the Lord's "controversy with the
inhabitants of the land." Hosea then portrays the complete
collapse of spiritual and moral life. Verse 2 sets out an "ugly
catalogue of sins"[1] typical of any decadent age, including our
own. This is followed in verse 3 by the ecological effects of
humanity's sin, a "picture of a poisoned environment."[2] Next

the religious leaders, both prophets and priests, come in for criticism, and they will be punished along with the people they are supposed to lead (vv. 4-9). Their minds are dulled by alcohol (v. 11) and superstition (v. 12) and they have become sex-crazed (vv. 12-18). All this leads inevitably to God's judgement and threats of punishment of which there are many expressions:

Judgment pertains to you. (5:1)

Woe to them, for they have strayed from me! Destruction to them, for they have rebelled against me! (7:13)

My anger burns against them. (8:5)

I will send a fire upon his cities, and it shall devour his strongholds. (8:14 RSV)

Hosea also proclaims God's love for Israel and this involves a tension in the heart of God. It is movingly portrayed in chapter 11. God is a Father, and Israel (against whom his anger burns) is his son whom he loves (v. 1) But Israel spurned that love (v. 2) Yet God has continued to bestow a father's love upon them: "It was I who taught Ephraim to walk, taking them by the arms; but they did not realize it was I who healed them. I led them with cords of human kindness, with ties of love; I lifted the yoke from their neck, and bent down to feed them" (v. 4).

Israel is therefore worthy of judgment and verses 5-7 describe how it would come at the hand of Assyria. But then the Father's love protests against this expression of his wrath: "How can I give you up, Ephraim? How can I hand you over, Israel? My heart is changed within me; all my compassion is aroused. I will not carry out my fierce anger, nor will I turn and devastate Ephraim. For I am God and not man—the Holy One among you. I will not come in wrath" (vv. 8-9).

How are we to express this tension in God's heart? Not by an anemic view of God's judgment against sin combined with an inhibited expression of his love, but by an uncompromising witness to both. Yet to maintain such a balance of truth is never easy, especially between the wrath and love of God. How was Hosea enabled to do it? It was through the lessons he painfully learned from coping with his unfaithful wife, whose behavior was a perfect replica of what God had to endure from Israel.

## Hosea's Marriage

Three children were born, all of whom were given significant names which reflected what was going on in Israel. First there was Jezreel, which means "God scatters," a reference to God's judgment. It will be remembered that the town of that name was the place of Jehu's blood-bath, an extreme violence which Israel had never repudiated. The next, "Not pitied" or, no longer an object of mercy, revealed Hosea's rising suspicion about his wife's immorality. Indeed it seems likely that Hosea was not the father, for it does not say that she bore him a daughter, but simply that she conceived (Hos 1:6). The third was called "Not my people" and speaks of complete estrangement, because this time Hosea was clearly not the father.

As with Hosea's marriage, so with Israel—the sovereignty of God is unimpaired. His purposes (1:10) first revealed to Abraham cannot be frustrated. The solemn state of affairs indicated by the names of the children would be reversed (1:10—2:1). "Where it was said to them, 'You are not my people,' they will be called 'sons of the living God' " (v. 10).

But God cannot take lightly the behavior of Israel any more than Hosea can turn a blind eye to his wife's conduct. So before returning to his intention to reverse the three names (2:23), Hosea first spells out the kind of punishment that befits adultery, referring first to his wife and then slipping into language which describes the spiritual adultery of the nation (2:2-13). He is making out a legal case. "Plead" (2:2 RSV) is the kind of contending that takes place in a court of law and has the same root as "controversy" (4:1 RSV).

"The punishment of verses 9-13 [chapter 2] is unsparing, yet not unjust; in fact, as the sequel will show in 14ff., far from unfeeling."[3] For God is not only a prosecutor seeking justice, but a husband who loves his wife and, no matter how she may have behaved, is determined to keep his side of the marriage covenant. So he expresses his intention by the repeated use of the words "I will." First it is "I will allure her" because, as Kidner comments, "true love need be no less ravishing than false."[4] His supreme aim is to restore the marriage covenant, and so "I will betroth you" repeats three times in verses 19-20, leading to the promise to reinstate his people which is indicated by reversing the names of the children.

Is it, then, only necessary to "allure her" and "speak tenderly to her" (2:14) to restore Israel to all that was promised "in the day she came up out of Egypt" (v. 15), returning to the Lord to call him "my husband" (v. 16)? It isn't as easy as that. Even when Israel responds to God's call to repentance, there is still a price to be paid, and Hosea was to learn this lesson in a way which would print it indelibly on his heart. When he went after his erring wife, he discovered that she had become a slave concubine to another man—a striking picture of Israel's apostasy (3:1). But he loved her just the same, even to the extent of paying a price to get her back (v. 2).

We cannot fail to see here a reflection, even if only a faint one, of Calvary. When God carries out his purpose to save his people from their sins, it is not enough for him to move them to repentance. There is a price to be paid—the shed blood of his Son. Forgiveness is not cheap. And, as Hosea discovered, there is always a price to be paid by those who are prepared to love sinners.

What did Hosea and what can we learn from this? It is to be hoped that none of us ever have to endure anything approaching what Hosea suffered. Yet all of us at some time sustain injury through living in a sinful world. The way we learn to cope with it may well be God's way of shaping us for the ministry he has for us, costly to us though it may prove to be.

This was the way Hosea gained an insight into the heart of God, who burns with wrath against humanity's sin, yet loves the sinner with an infinite love. As he underwent emotional torture at the hands of his wife, his mind, feelings and will were all shaped by it. When we suffer from unfaithfulness in another, may it help us to understand how God feels about our unfaithfulness. When we experience the hurt of children going against us and doing wrong, may it give us some idea of how God feels when we go against him.

Here is the twofold attitude which must be ours. Let us never lose our God-given sense of outrage at the sins of humanity. When we cease to be shocked by sin, we lose one of our important defenses against it. At the same time we love those for whom Christ died, even though we are frustrated by their unbelief and low moral standards. How can we be used to bring conviction of sin to others? In our own lives we must learn to be uncompromising with sin—like Hosea who had to take a strong line with his wife. How can we effectively proclaim God's love and forgiveness? By being forgiving ourselves, even to the extent of paying the price of the sins of others, as did Hosea when he bought his wife back, and as did God when he paid the price of our sins on the cross. The injuries which we suffer from this sinful world, not least those that arise in the setting of home and family, can mold and shape us, and make us more effective in showing forth both God's hatred of sin, and his love for the sinner.

## Questions for Individuals or Groups

1. When have you seen a dysfunctional home life create difficulties for someone in ministry? (pp. 95-97) What was the result?

2. Do you agree or disagree with the author's assessment of why God wanted Hosea to marry Gomer? (pp. 97-98, 102-3) Why or why not?

3. When have you seen the two approaches mentioned (hard and soft) at work in times of moral decay? (pp. 99-100)

4. How does Hosea's marriage help you to better understand God's dealing with Israel? (pp. 102-4)

5. How does Hosea's experience help you to understand the cost of salvation for God? (p. 104)

6. When have personal experiences of suffering helped you to minister to the needs of others?

# 7

# IMPULSIVENESS
## Peter

Is THERE ANY DIFFERENCE BETWEEN A NATURAL GIFT OF LEADER-
ship and what is required by Christian leaders? Should Christians who are gifted leaders in politics, the armed forces, sports,
business or one of the other professions be obvious choices for
positions of spiritual responsibility? Do those engaged in academic work necessarily possess a wisdom which qualifies them
for leadership in church work? Or are special qualities called
for? To find the answers to these questions about Christian
leadership we must look to Christ and not to secular sources
like management psychology.

Jesus was clearly recognizing a difference between leaders in
the world and what he was looking for in his disciples when
he pointed out to them, "You know that those who are re-

garded as rulers of the Gentiles lord it over them. Not so with
you" (Mk 10:42-43). He said that in response to the request for
prominence by James and John in which their mother had a
hand. They were displaying a love of power and status, a common human failing which needs to be faced up to by all who
aspire to leadership roles in the church. Sometimes persons in
an influential position in the world expect to receive the same
deference in their local churches. Or it can just as readily work
the other way. Failure to receive promotion in a secular occupation is compensated by seeking power in the church. Is this
why shared leadership can sometimes cause division? Is it because those who exercise it sometimes lack the ingredients
which are essential for spiritual leadership? Discord was certainly one of the effects of James and John seeking status, as
Matthew reports that when the ten heard it, "they were indignant with the two brothers" (Mt 20:24).

### Peter: A Natural Leader

The most outstanding example in the New Testament of a natural leader who was transformed into a spiritual one is Peter.
He has no sooner joined the band of disciples than he assumes
the leadership, and from then on his formidable figure dominates the scene. Next to our Lord himself the Gospel writers
refer to him more than anyone else. He has more to say, and
Jesus speaks oftener to him than any other disciple. If Jesus
asked a question, it was usually Peter who answered. If the
disciples had questions to raise, Peter was their spokesperson.

After the ascension, Peter and the other apostles took it for
granted that he was the one to take over the leadership. In
characteristic style "Peter stood up among the believers" (Acts
1:15) and took the initiative in replacing Judas Iscariot. On the
Day of Pentecost it was Peter who "stood up with the Eleven"

(Acts 2:14) and preached the first evangelistic sermon of this age. His leadership was also recognized outside the church, for the last we see of him in Acts is when Herod wanted to make an example of a leading member of the church and selected Peter.

The assessment of A. B. Bruce was that "both by his virtues and by his infirmities Peter was predestined to be the champion of the faith, the Luther of the apostolic age, giving and receiving the hardest blows, and bearing the brunt of the battle."[1] He was indeed a "born leader." It was a splendid day's work on the part of Andrew when he introduced him to Jesus, which William Temple thought to be "as great a service to the Church as ever any man did."[2] But was Peter's natural gift of leadership, which he brought with him into the church, suitable for what Jesus was planning for him?

Peter had certain limitations which would have to be taken into account. For one thing he did not come from the same social background as did most of the leaders in the world of those days. He was an uneducated fisherman and probably unable to read or write. Additionally, he may not have been as quick to see what was going on as some others. When visiting the tomb of Jesus on the first Easter morning, unlike John who "saw and believed" (Jn 20:8), he failed to see the significance of the graveclothes. His gifts were practical rather than intellectual, and he would have found it difficult to follow a reasoned argument. Yet none of these limitations was allowed to stand in the way of Peter's call to leadership.

He could fairly be described as a rough diamond. He could be violent if the situation seemed to demand it, as he did when he attacked the high priest's servant with a sword (Mt 26:52). His language could be quite coarse, as it was when he was trying to make his denial that he even knew Jesus sound convincing—and that was after he had been a disciple for three years. And this was the man who became one of the most outstanding leaders of the New Testament church.

Peter certainly took some handling. His good points and bad ones, his successes and failures, were all larger than life. His discipleship was a tempestuous affair. There was the occasion when he nearly got more than his feet wet through trying to walk on the sea. At one point Jesus was congratulating him on his God-given insight and a moment later was rebuking him for expressing opinions which he attributed to Satan. In the Upper Room Jesus had to show him the door when he argued over the foot washing. A few hours later, after protestations of loyalty, he denied that he had ever known Jesus. After the Ascension, his life in the early church was far from smooth. He was still arguing with the Lord when he reluctantly went to meet the Gentile, Cornelius, and later, in Antioch he received a rebuke from Paul for inconsistent conduct.

**An Impulsive Personality**
The facet of his personality which most determined his style of leadership was his impetuosity. No one could have been with Peter for long, before coming up against it. What so often made him difficult to cope with was his habit of speaking or acting without so much as a brief pause for thought. If a course of action seemed right, he would pursue it without delay. A typical example of his impulsive nature was when he was in a boat and went clean overboard in his eagerness to reach Jesus whom he had just recognized.

He was quick-tempered and at times quite arrogant. If he had strong feelings on any matter, he expressed them. As a consequence, he had the unfortunate habit of blurting out remarks which would have been better left unsaid. His reaction to the

Transfiguration was to say the first thing that came into his head (Mk 9:5). Mark comments, perhaps having found out directly from Peter, "he did not know what to say" (Mk 9:6) but, being Peter, he had to say something. Worst of all, Peter's impulsive speech could make him into a tool of the devil as when Jesus had to say to him: "Get behind me, Satan! You do not have in mind the things of God, but the things of men" (Mk 8:33).

At the same time an impulsive personality can make a helpful contribution to natural gifts of leadership. Quick decisions which are put into effect with enthusiasm can provide just the inspiration which the group needs. But it is essential that such decisions are as wise as they are speedy. A responsible leader must learn to speak and act after careful thought and needs to develop a sound judgment. Impulsive remarks made without thought can have far reaching repercussions to be regretted for a long time.

Preachers need to be careful about additions made to their sermons on the spur of the moment which are not in their notes but arise from their feelings while in the pulpit. They are not necessarily the promptings of the Holy Spirit! Pastors must not react to those they are seeking to help without listening carefully to their problems and then giving due thought to the advice they give. Likewise, committee chairpersons must not give way to their feelings, but use their minds when views which irritate them are expressed in committee.

### Spiritual Leadership

What extra qualities, then, are needed for spiritual leadership? A study of the way our Lord related to Peter reveals four qualities. The first is humility. This must replace the assertiveness which impulsive persons like Peter will use in expressing their opinions. The need for it is exemplified by Peter in the way he did not hesitate to correct Jesus. He even did this just after he had expressed his conviction that Jesus was the Messiah. He made bold assertions of loyalty, comparing himself very favorably with the other disciples, but was quite oblivious of his own weakness which led to his downfall.

Second, he needed to submit himself to the authority of Jesus and be willing to learn from him. Those who would be leaders of others in the church must first become disciples. Submission to Jesus called also for a third requirement—faith in him. Spiritual leaders must be persons of faith if they are going to command the respect of others and gain their confidence. This was one of the strengths of leaders like Paul, whose deep faith in Christ lay behind the conviction with which he spoke. He found a verse in the Psalms to demonstrate this: " 'I believed; therefore I have spoken.' With that same spirit of faith we also believe, and therefore speak" (2 Cor 4:13).

Then fourth, a Christian leader needs the gift of love expressed both toward God and in ministry toward others. Leadership in the church is more than the ability to run an organization successfully. Preaching which is going to feed the flock is more than the intellectual satisfaction of expounding fascinating themes. What then has the life of Peter to teach us about how these qualities can be developed?

A frequent answer is to point to Pentecost and the difference it made to Peter and the other apostles. That event undoubtedly proved to be a turning point in Peter's life, and many sermons have been rightly preached contrasting him before and after. But to see it as the only factor is a simplistic view of the way God deals with us, overlooking what Jesus did for Peter during his earthly ministry. Those three years were largely devoted to what A. B. Bruce described as "The Training of the Twelve."

All the time Peter was learning along with the other disciples but, in addition, there was a series of incidents with Peter at the center. Many of them were quite critical in nature, in which Peter learned largely from his mistakes, but he emerged from them all the better equipped for the spiritual demands which lay ahead of him.

In these lessons Peter made an encouraging start. An outstanding example is what happened after Jesus had preached to the Galilean crowds from his boat. Jesus told him to "put out into deep water, and let down the nets for a catch" (Lk 5:4). Peter's answer was first to tell Jesus that they had been out all night with no success. He might well have pointed out that in these circumstances it was useless to try again in broad daylight with the morning sun glistening on the water. In any case an experienced fisherman like Peter knew more about it than a carpenter. What Peter actually said to Jesus was a fine example of submission for he continued, "But because you say so, I will let down the nets" (Lk 5:5). Even though what Jesus said was contrary to all that Peter's expertise told him, he accepted it. This shows how the seeds of faith had already been implanted in him through his first encounters with Jesus. Alan Stibbs has cited this as a practical expression of an important principle: "Critical inquiry and honest investigation are right and commendable as a means to discover the truth about Jesus. But once I know who he is, once I have reached the place where evidence demands that I recognise him as trustworthy, then he asks nothing less than uncompromising and unconditional loyalty."[3]

On this occasion another quality which Peter would need to develop made its appearance—humility. His submission to Jesus was accompanied by a humble assessment of himself. In response to the miraculous catch of fish which resulted from his obedience to Jesus he "fell at Jesus' knees and said, 'Go away from me, Lord; I am a sinful man!' " (Lk 5:8). Instead of impulsively rushing into an offer of service after such an outstanding demonstration of power by Jesus, his only thought was of his own unworthiness to serve such a master. Here, Peter was aligning himself with the great people of God in the Bible who initially responded to the call to spiritual leadership with the same reticence. It was before such an attitude that Jesus gave Peter the commission, "Don't be afraid; from now on you will catch men" (Lk 5:10). That was enough for Peter and the other disciples: "So they pulled their boats up on shore, left everything and followed him" (Lk 5:11).

All this, however, was only a beginning. Peter had to continue to develop these qualities when the novelty of following Jesus had worn off. This encouraging initial response would have to be tested, nurtured and applied in a variety of circumstances. If his impulsive nature was to be refined, the qualifications for spiritual leadership would have to take deep root in his personality.

**Lessons in Faith**
The very next incident reveals a deficiency in Peter's faith which would have to be mended. It was the occasion when the disciples were in a boat and saw Jesus walking on the sea. Once Peter realized who it was, his immediate reaction was the desire to do the same. If Jesus was master over the sea and a stormy sea at that, then Peter wanted to share in that. It was surely an act of faith for Peter, once Jesus had given him the go-ahead, to step out of the boat on to the sea. Yet, the story reveals that there is more to faith than rushing thoughtlessly into an exciting exploit. When he saw the wind, "he was afraid, and beginning to sink, cried out, 'Lord, save me' " (Mt 14:30). Jesus came

to his rescue, calling him a man of "little faith" (Mt 14:31).

Mercifully, our salvation does not depend on the strength of our faith. "Jesus often rebukes weak faith," observed John Berridge, an eighteenth-century evangelical leader, "but never rejects it."[4] For progress in the Christian life and effective service, however, faith of a stronger calibre is required. The Old Testament heroes listed in Hebrews 11, who "conquered kingdoms" (v. 33) and overcame all the obstacles detailed in the following verses were without exception characterized by the strength of their faith. The "little faith" which Peter possessed was enough to begin a relationship with Christ, but it could not withstand the wind and the waves of the sea, nor would it be sufficient for the pressures which were to come upon the young church he was destined to lead.

The way that some young people contemplate full-time Christian service and leadership is not unlike Peter's romantic ideas of walking on the sea. The atmosphere of a chorus-singing youth fellowship does not necessarily demand a particularly well-thought-out faith. But the challenge of secular thought and the issues raised by theological study in a university can be as much a challenge to faith as the cold winds that Peter had to face. Loneliness, too, which is the portion of many Christian leaders, demands a faith which is truly one's own, and which can survive when all earthly props are taken away. There may also be persecution to face, as Peter soon discovered when Jesus took them to Jerusalem for his suffering and death. But, as Peter himself was to write many years later, such trials will prove whether faith is genuine; it is being tested and refined by fire like a precious metal (2 Pet 1:7).

One of the aims of our Lord's ministry to his disciples was to lead them from their initial belief in him to an intelligent and mature faith which was based on a clear understanding of who he was. Peter reached that stage toward the end of Jesus' Galilean ministry, and it is demonstrated by two incidents, one recorded in the Gospels.

The first one follows the feeding of the five thousand and the discourse about the bread of life. A number of defections among the disciples prompted Jesus to ask the Twelve if any of them were contemplating doing the same. There was good reason for posing such a question. After all, it had been one thing to be a disciple when crowds were following Jesus, but a very different affair in the chilly atmosphere of disillusionment which now prevailed. Peter's reply was unequivocal: "Lord, to whom shall we go? You have the words of eternal life. We believe and know that you are the Holy One of God" (Jn 6:68-69).

He recognized that eternal life was to be found in Jesus and nowhere else, and in calling him "The Holy One of God" he was using language reminiscent of the Old Testament way of referring to Jehovah as "the Holy One of Israel." Although at this stage, Peter would hardly have been able to give a theological statement of the deity of Christ, what he said shows that he had reached a very high view of the person of Jesus. Furthermore, the use of the perfect tense implies that Peter had reached a settled faith. Leon Morris suggests as a translation, "We have come to a place of faith and continue there. We have entered into knowledge and retain it."[5]

The example found in the other Gospels occurred a little later at Caesarea Philippi. Jesus had taken the disciples to a quiet place far removed from the crowds of Galilee and, having asked them for an account of the popular views about himself, he asked, "Who do you say I am?" (Mt 16:15). Although it is typical of Peter's impulsive nature to speak without stopping to think, this time he did not need to. Ever since his brother Andrew had first introduced him to Jesus with the declaration,

"We have found the Messiah," he had been observing him at close quarters, hearing his teaching and assessing his divine claims. His spontaneous reply shows the conviction he had reached.

Matthew gives the fullest account of Peter's reply: "You are the Christ, the Son of the living God" (Mt 16:16). This was the moment Jesus chose to repeat his new name "Peter" meaning "a rock," which he had given him when they first met (Jn 1:42). A few days later Peter was given further evidence of the person of Christ at the transfiguration. He was one of a chosen few who "were eyewitnesses of his majesty" when they "were with him on the sacred mountain" (2 Pet 1:16-18), as he wrote many years later.

It is true that there were misunderstandings to be cleared up before the Holy Spirit led Peter and the other Apostles "into all the truth" (Jn 16:13). Also there was failure ahead when Peter denied all knowledge of Jesus. But, tragic though it was, it proved to be only a temporary lapse and, aided by the prayers of Jesus, his growing faith remained intact as Jesus promised, "I have prayed for you, Simon, that your faith may not fail" (Lk 22:32). The Resurrection provided further confirmation that Peter's faith in the person of Christ was well founded. By then he was ready for Pentecost and all that followed.

Here is what surely ought to lie at the heart of the faith of every Christian leader—a deep conviction about the person of our Lord. Like the first Christian leaders, we must hold this on strong objective grounds. It will be the key to everything else we believe. We will, for example, accept the inspiration and reliability of the Old Testament, ultimately because Jesus did. We may suffer many disappointments in our ministry and sometimes feel let down by others, but the facts about Christ are never called into question.

## Lessons in Submission

When Peter had made his confession of faith at Caesarea Philippi, it might have been assumed that the way was now open for him to make great strides as a Christian disciple and a future church leader. There was, however, a further lesson for Peter to learn—to submit himself completely to the authority of Jesus. And that was far from easy, as it involved accepting what Jesus said about his approaching death on a Roman gallows, an idea which he and the other disciples found utterly repugnant. All of the first three gospels are quite specific in saying it was immediately after Peter's confession that Jesus began to show his disciples that he must go to Jerusalem and suffer many things from the elders and chief priests and scribes, and be killed, and on the third day be raised (Mt 16:21). Peter's reaction was predictable. He did not hesitate to contradict Jesus, even though he had just declared him to be the Messiah: "Never, Lord! This shall never happen to you!" (Mt 16:22).

We need not doubt that there were commendable motives underlying his protest and that his great concern was to deflect Jesus from a suicidal visit to Jerusalem. The fact remains, however, that Peter had the audacity to correct one whom he had just confessed to be "the Christ, the Son of the living God" (Mt 16:16). Peter had not yet taken in the only possible consequence of such a view of Jesus, which was humbly to submit to what he said, even though it was far beyond his understanding. But Peter presumed to put Jesus right and in doing so he was rejecting the cross, which was the supreme purpose of Jesus' coming into the world. Mercifully Jesus did not say "Get behind me, Peter!" That would have meant the end of Peter's discipleship. What he did say was, "Get behind me, Satan!" (Mt 16:23), recognizing that the devil would make full use of Peter's impetuosity and lack of understanding.

It was essentially the same issue that was at stake in the Upper Room when Peter refused to let Jesus wash his feet. By this action Jesus was assuming the role of the servant of the Lord who was to give his life as a ransom, but Peter persisted in his rejection of that kind of a Messiah. Jesus assured Peter that he even though he did not understand at the time, later he would. Peter remained adamant: "You shall never wash my feet" (Jn 13:8). But Jesus was equally determined.

Peter's obstinacy had gone far enough and the whole issue must be brought to a head. What he said was in effect that if Peter persisted in rejecting what he was seeking to teach by word and action, then he could not continue as a disciple. He had to accept Jesus as the suffering servant of the Lord, or not at all. "Unless I wash you," he warned him, "you have no part with me" (Jn 13:8). Jesus knew Peter well enough to know what his reaction would be. His spontaneous reply left no doubt as to where Peter ultimately stood, "Then, Lord, not just my feet, but my hands and my head as well!" (Jn 13:9). And for one who made such a complete submission to his Master, it proved later to be just as Jesus had foreseen: "later you will understand" (Jn 13:7).

## A Lesson in Humility

Why did Peter experience such difficulty in submitting to Jesus even though he believed him to be the Son of God? One reason was that he had not yet learned the humility which is an essential of truly spiritual leadership. His self-confidence needed to be replaced by a more humble assessment of his own unaided wisdom and understanding. The kind of leadership that God looks for cannot coexist with arrogance and self-assertion.

This trait in Peter's character makes Jesus' response to his confession all the more pertinent. While some who rejected

Jesus' divine claims were Peter's intellectual superiors, that proved to be of no advantage to them when confronted by the uncompromising claims of Jesus. The reason Peter recognized the truth about Jesus was not because of his intelligence and insight, as Jesus said: "This was not revealed to you by man, but by my Father in heaven" (Mt 16:17). If it had been left to Peter's unaided wisdom, he would never have come to a right understanding of Jesus.

The same can be said of Paul. He needed a special revelation on the Damascus road. Of those who fail to appreciate the truth of the gospel he wrote, "The god of this age has blinded the minds of unbelievers, so that they cannot see the light of the gospel of the glory of Christ" (2 Cor 4:4). How then does anyone come to "see the light of the gospel"? Paul's explanation is quite clear: "For God, who said, 'Let light shine out of darkness' made his light shine in our hearts to give us the light of the knowledge of the glory of God in the face of Christ" (2 Cor 4:6). This means that all who, like Peter, have come to faith in Christ, must regard this as a ground not for self-congratulation, but for humbly thanking God that he has revealed his truth to an otherwise darkened mind.

It was Peter's denial of Jesus that gave him the humbling that he so desperately needed. Jesus warned him in advance that it would happen, but Peter could not believe it and responded with a promise of loyalty which is recorded in all four Gospels. He even claimed a devotion to Christ which exceeded that of the other apostles. There is no need to doubt that Peter sincerely meant what he said, but he had not taken his own weakness into account.

It is true that Peter was quite prepared to draw a sword in an attempt to defend Jesus against considerable human odds. In that context he was no coward. But he had not considered how he would cope with the sneer of a servant girl. By a skillful use of Greek, John shows how Peter allowed himself to be maneuvered into a compromised position. The girl's question expected the answer no, so, by saying very little, Peter could leave her with the impression that he was no disciple of Jesus. This must have seemed reasonable enough, for you would not have expected to find a disciple of the prisoner in the court of the high priest. When the question was repeated later, it again anticipated the answer no, and this time Peter responded, so Matthew and Mark tell us, with oaths and curses.

Unfortunately for Peter, the third questioner knew quite well who he was because he was related to the one who had been at the sharp end of Peter's sword and had been present at the time. He readily recognized Peter and issued a straight challenge that he had seen him in the Garden of Gethsemane—Matthew and Mark added that Peter's Galilean accent gave him away. This time the questioner was looking for the answer yes. The moment had come for Peter to stand up and be counted. But that would have meant going back on the impression he had given to the first questioner. So he flatly denied all knowledge of Jesus (Jn 18:15-18, 25-27), with oaths and curses (Mt 26:74). Then the cock crowed reminding Peter of what Jesus had predicted, and when Jesus' eyes met his, he slipped into the darkness outside with tears streaming down his cheeks (Lk 22:61-62).

Peter had now reached his lowest point. But it proved to be the upturn which Jesus had foreseen. Here was practical evidence of Peter's weakness, which he could never explain away. At the same time he saw Jesus as a complete contrast to himself. Although he could not yet understand the cross, it was now only too clear that Jesus was intent on going through with it. What impressed him was the humility with which Jesus bore his sufferings, as he was later to stress (1 Pet 2:19-21). Moreover, when he was setting before church leaders the qualities, including humility, to be expected of them, he wrote as "a witness of Christ's sufferings" (1 Pet 5:1).

For the next encounter Peter had with Jesus we rely on the simple statement recorded by Luke, "The Lord has risen and has appeared to Simon!" (Lk 24:34). We are not told what passed between them. We can only make the safe guess that Peter seized the opportunity to express his deep regret for what had happened and that Jesus freely forgave him. What is clear is that at their next meeting the relationship had been restored, for Peter does not behave like a guilty man.

That next encounter took place on the beach of the Sea of Galilee where the disciples who had been fishers returned to their previous occupation, but without success. When they followed the suggestion of a lone figure on the shore to have another try, the large catch must have reminded one of them, presumably John, of a similar happening three years earlier, for he recognized the stranger. No sooner had he said to Peter, "It is the Lord," than his companion was in the sea on his way to meet Jesus.

Peter's action shows that he still had the same impulsive personality, but the conversation which followed showed a significant change in his character. Three times Jesus asks him, "Simon son of John, do you truly love me more than these?" (Jn 21:15). John uses here the verb *agapao*, but for Peter's reply he uses the weaker word *phileo*. Peter has lost the arrogance which had characterized him and shrinks from claiming the highest kind of love Jesus was asking for. In his first question Jesus adds "more than these." The most likely explanation of this phrase is that Jesus had in mind Peter's earlier claim to loyalty which surpassed the other disciples. But Peter's failure

had served to rid him of that kind of arrogance and the brag-
ging spirit with which he had expressed it. So he simply affirmed his love without any boastful comparisons with others.

While Peter is not able to point to any practical evidence in
his life to enforce his profession of love for Jesus, he appeals
to Jesus' perfect knowledge of him by prefixing "you know" to
each reply. Having the same question put to him three times
must have reminded him of the number of times he had denied
Jesus. But there is no trace of the indignation we might have
expected from our earlier picture of Peter. Rather we are told
that he "was hurt because Jesus asked him the third time, 'Do
you love me?' " (Jn 21:17).

Here is evidence of the change taking place in Peter, fitting
him for spiritual leadership. So Jesus saw that he was now ready
for the threefold commission: "Feed my lambs"; "Tend my
sheep"; "Feed my sheep" (Jn 21:15-17 RSV). A. B. Bruce has
concluded: "The man who can so take allusions to his sins is
not only fit to tend the sheep, but even to nurse the lambs. He
will restore those who have fallen in a spirit of meekness. He
will be tender toward offenders, not with the spurious charity
which cannot afford to condemn sin strongly, but with the
genuine charity of one who has himself received mercy for sins
sincerely repented of."[6]

## A Lesson in Love

We see how different the natural gift of leadership is from spiritual leadership, which is characterized by faith in Christ, submission to him and a humble view of oneself! There is a quality
which distinguishes the two kinds of leadership still further. It
is expressed by the simple question Jesus put three times to
Peter, "Do you love me?" This question is of particular relevance
to anyone whose leadership style is highly organizational.

A gift for organizing seems to have accompanied Peter's impetuosity. He had already shown a readiness to organize his fellow disciples, and he continued to do this in the early days of the Jerusalem church. It was Peter who decided that the number of the Apostles should be increased to twelve again by finding a replacement for Judas Iscariot.

But people who enjoy organizing and take pleasure in seeing a work being built up under their leadership, need to be reminded that they are not to find satisfaction simply out of seeing their work run like a well-oiled machine. Rather, all that they undertake is to be out of love for their Master. Paul stresses this requirement in a well-known chapter, where he insists that without love all of our gifts are useless (1 Cor 13:1-3).

The terms in which Jesus describes Peter's future ministry also has a bearing on what the capable organizer must keep in mind. He had first spoken of it as fishing for disciples (Lk 5:10). He now employs another metaphor as he says to Peter, "Feed my lambs." Peter was to think of his future work in pastoral terms, for the church is not a machine but a flock, not an organization but an organism and its members are people. And although efficient organizing is good for the church, the supreme task of its leaders is not to organize, but to feed.

That concludes the training which Peter received during the earthly ministry of our Lord. Along with the other apostles, he received the final commission immediately before the Ascension. He shared with them the outpouring of the Holy Spirit giving power for service as Jesus had promised. We then see him fully exercising his gifts of leadership, both in witness before the world and in care for the church. But it is a very different Peter from the one we have met in the Gospels. At the Council of Jerusalem in Acts 15 he did not speak until the others had. In Mark's Gospel which (according to many schol-

ars) records the preaching of Peter, there is no attempt to glorify him. Indeed, events which give prominence to Peter are
played down, while some of those which are derogatory of him
are recorded in detail. This contrasts many Christian speakers
and authors who manage to find examples from their past
experience which, not only illustrate their theme, but glorify
themselves at the same time.

The place in the New Testament, however, where we find
most clearly what Peter had learned about leadership is the
passage in his first epistle which is addressed to the elders
among his readers. It is written with a humility which is far
removed from the self-assertiveness of his earlier years. Cranfield sees it as "the humility and gentleness of one who once
was self-reliant and impetuous, but has been chastened and
refined."[7]

He first connects with his readers by describing himself as
a "fellow elder" (1 Pet 5:1), and enjoins them: "Clothe yourselves with humility toward one another, because, 'God opposes
the proud, but gives grace to the humble' " (v. 5). He also shows
that he has absorbed into his style of leadership its pastoral
nature which Jesus had taught him, describing the church as
"God's flock" (v. 2). Perhaps remembering rulers in the Old
Testament who were likened to unfaithful shepherds—more
concerned with feeding themselves than the flock—he reminds
the elders that the flock is not theirs. It is "God's flock that is
under your care" (v. 2), and it is to the "Chief Shepherd" (v. 4)
that the elders must look for their reward.

Underlying such a ministry there must be the right motives,
and these Peter describes as three pairs of contrasts (v. 2-3). First,
ministry is to be carried out "not because you must, but because
you are willing." As an example of the wrong kind of motive,
Cranfield suggests social pressure which can easily force a per-

son into ministry (for instance, when everybody assumes that the minister's children will follow their father) "and the same sort of thing can happen with other forms of pastoral responsibility."[8] The love of material gain is likewise to be spurned. The true pastor will tend the flock "not for shameful gain but eagerly." The third pitfall against which Peter warns is "domineering over those in your charge" (v. 3 RSV). The way for spiritual leaders to operate is not from the carnal ability to impose their will on others, but by "being examples to the flock."

We have seen how Jesus shaped Peter for the style of leadership which suits the work of the gospel. But his supreme qualification for addressing his fellow elders on this subject is that he was "a witness of Christ's sufferings" (1 Pet 5:1). Having resisted any suggestion that the Messiah was to suffer death, when it actually happened, it made a lasting impression on him and profoundly influenced his understanding of Christian leadership. The epistle shows not only that Peter had come to understand the meaning of Christ's death, but also had been deeply moved by the way he faced it.

Peter found in Christ the perfect demonstration of the kind of ministry which he demands from the leaders of his church. Peter had heard him say, when answering the request of James and John to be given prominent positions in glory, "Whoever wants to be first must be slave of all. For even the Son of Man did not come to be served, but to serve, and to give his life as a ransom for many" (Mk 10:44-45). That is far removed from much of the leadership style we find in the world, but is indispensible in the church, as we shall see in the next chapter.

## Questions for Individuals or Groups

1. Describe an impulsive person you have known. How did others react to him or her?

2. Have you ever worked with an impulsive leader? What were the benefits

of working with this personality type? the drawbacks? (pp. 110-11)

3. How do you differentiate the qualities of a natural leader from a spiritual one? (pp. 108-9, 111-14)

4. What contemporary situations do Christian leaders face which require an extra measure of faith? (p. 115)

5. Why was it important for Peter to allow Jesus to wash his feet? (p. 119) What did Jesus want to teach him about leadership?

6. Why do you think that the author says, "the kind of leadership that God looks for cannot coexist with arrogance and self-assertion?" (pp. 119-20) What would be the result of prideful leadership?

7. What changes in Peter are revealed in his response to Jesus' questions? (pp. 122-23)

8. What kinds of experiences have you had working with persons who have a gift for organizing? Do you agree with the author that they must be reminded "not to organize but to feed?" (pp. 124-25) Why or why not?

9. How do Peter's letters reveal what he has learned about leadership? (pp. 125-26)

10. What significance does the leadership model described in the final paragraph have for you in your ministry?

# 8

# THE LOVE OF POWER
# AND PRESTIGE

## James and John

CLOSELY ASSOCIATED WITH PETER WERE JAMES AND JOHN, WHO shared with him the distinction of being in the inner circle of disciples. The three were, for example, the only ones allowed to witness the raising of Jairus' daughter (Mk 5:37), to be present at the transfiguration (Mk 9:2) and to be chosen to accompany Jesus during his agony in Gethsemane (Mk 14:33). There is no apparent evidence, however, that Peter shared the love of power and prestige which they displayed for all to see when they blatantly asked Jesus, "Let one of us sit at your right and the other at your left in your glory" (Mk 10:37).

What gave them such ideas? Perhaps the privileges they had been granted had gone to their heads. Sometimes people who are often in a leadership role begin to assume that it is theirs by right, and find it difficult to take a backseat. Another possible contribution was a feeling that they were socially superior to the other disciples, as their father could afford hired servants (Mk 1:20). (A modern equivalent are those who assume that, because they live in a big house and are able to make substantial financial contributions, they ought always to be consulted on church matters.) Also it seems that John was socially well connected—assuming he was the other disciple in the courtyard with Jesus and Peter—because he "was known to the high priest" (Jn 18:15). Another very likely factor was the influence of their mother, since Matthew reveals that she also declared the same ambition for her sons (Mt 20:21). Now it is not unusual for a mother to take a pride in her sons and there can be something attractive about it. But to give them exaggerated ideas of their own importance is likely to prove a stumbling block. (Here ministers should take note that they don't allow their own children always to be the center of attention.)

### Desire for Power

Whatever the cause, the love of prestige and power is by no means uncommon among Christian leaders today. They can so easily become like "Diotrophes, who loves to be first" (3 Jn 9). Such a desire is a recipe for jealousy toward others who are potential rivals for the lead role, like the well-known preacher who declined to speak at a conference because he thought he was being asked to play second fiddle to another speaker.

Many years ago, I was greatly helped and challenged by a book by H. Guntrip which contained the following warning about preaching: "Few vocations can so subtly lay a man open to insincerity, egotism, over-estimation of his own importance and wisdom, intellectual and moral arrogance masked and disguised as religious fervour and conviction."[1] Persons who enjoy preaching, and being six feet above contradiction, more than other less public aspects of ministry ought to examine their motives carefully. Those who lay down the law in the pulpit on matters over which Bible-loving Christians differ, and question the integrity, learning or sanity of those who take a different view, ought to ask what impression they give to others. I have heard of a Roman Catholic who expressed preference for an infallible Pope confined to Rome rather than one in every pulpit!

Similar observations could probably be made of any occupation which exposes people to the public eye and in which success depends on winning the admiration of others, such as show-business stars, actors and musicians. A Christian actor once confided to me that one of his greatest problems was to reconcile his ambition to be a public success with the attitude to self demanded in the New Testament. And, as I have heard it said, the step from the stage to the pulpit is but a small one. Not that this is a danger which is confined to those who occupy pulpits. Plays, for example, when introduced into church services (whatever one's view of its place there) brings with it temptations of self-display, which militate against the atmosphere of worship. My own experience of it, in Britain at least, leads me to ask why plays always have to be funny, even when the biblical incidents enacted are anything but amusing in their original context.

All those in leadership positions in a local church will be well advised to watch themselves for signs that they enjoy the prestige that their office gives them. I recall a church official whose duties frequently meant that he had to walk up and down the aisle both before and during a service. It was disturbing to hear his perambulations described as "strutting around the church like a peacock. Additionally, someone who had a lot to do with clerical appointments in the Church of England once shared with me his experience of church wardens who, after a number of years in office, become "power crazy." I have heard something similar said about the secretary of a Baptist church. Work among young people is another area of Christian ministry which has its pitfalls, when it depends for its success on the leaders being heroes among their youthful followers.

Traveling can add to prestige. A visit to the United States can be a useful prestige builder for British clergy and can do for them what a preaching tour in Europe can do for Americans! Then, there is the prestige of sitting on as many committees as possible. Richard Lovelace claims, "It has been said of some religious leaders that they have the unusual ability to be able to strut sitting down."[2]

Academic achievement can go to a person's head, especially if it follows an earlier life in more humble circumstances. Those who seek academic distinction because of awareness that knowledge itself is power (Francis Bacon) must remember that it also "puffs up," as Paul had to warn the Corinthians. In the past evangelicals have often been despised for lack of scholarship. Happily this has been rectified, but the motive behind the pursuit of academic degrees needs always to be examined.

Of course, all this can easily be confused with the natural ambition to be a success. But what constitutes success? James Packer, in a timely editorial in *Christianity Today,* has warned of the danger of worshiping numerical success and regarding numerical growth as the chief validation of a ministry, with much time spent on studying and applying the right techniques and procedures. He is not against numerical growth as such, provided it is "qualitative as well as quantitative." But, he continues, "when numerical growth is idolized, so that churches and their clergy get rated failure for not achieving enough of it, my heart sinks."[3] He calls it "this secular passion for successful expansion." This reminds us of Elijah, whose depression, we discovered, arose partly from the failure to be the outstanding success he desired to be, like many business persons today. Indeed, the love of status which success brings is a common vice in the business world according to the observation of Peter Drucker: "The greatest time waster for most executives is a decision that has to do with someone's status. A move into new offices for example stirs up guerilla warfare as to who gets which office."[4]

Preoccupation with one's own reputation is bound to militate against the uplifting of Christ. Paul claimed, "For we do not preach ourselves, but Jesus Christ as Lord" (2 Cor 4:5). It was James Denney who once pointed out: "No man can ever bear witness to himself and Jesus Christ at one and the same time. No man, at one and the same time, can convey the impression that he himself is clever and that Christ is mighty to save." As John the Baptist corrected those who were jealous for his reputation, "He must become greater; I must become less" (Jn 3:30).

### The Marks of True Greatness

Many of us, if we are honest, enjoy a share of power and prestige. How then did Jesus respond to the request of James and John? The most direct answer is in Mark 10:40—positions of prominence are Christ's to give, but are given according to the Father's will and under his sovereignty. But the lesson which receives the fullest treatment concerns the nature of true greatness, as shown by two of its features.

First, it is costly. He pointed out to them that if they wanted to share his throne, they must also walk with him on the path which leads to it. This would involve sharing the cup he was to drink and the baptism he was to undergo, clear references to the humiliating death that was ahead of him (Mk 10:38). Jesus had been predicting it as he made his way to Jerusalem to face it, which just shows how insensitive they were to give vent to their grandiose ideas at such a time. But there is also an irony about their request which we can appreciate with the gift of hindsight, "in that those on the right and left of the Lord at the great moment of His triumph were two crucified thieves."[5] Questioned by Jesus as to whether they were ready to tread such a path, they assured him that they were. Whether or not that was a thoughtful reply is hard to say, but Jesus could see that it was indeed the price that they would pay for their allegiance to him. And so it proved to be. From Pentecost onward they were persecuted by the Jerusalem authorities until "King Herod arrested some who belonged to the church, intending to persecute them. He had James, the brother of John, put to death with the sword" (Acts 12:1-2).

This has often been the price of prominence. During the war of 1914-1918, it was said that to become a commissioned officer in the infantry was a death warrant, as snipers always picked off those who were obviously officers. It has been the same with most persecutions of the Christian church from New Testament days to the present time. Would those who love prominence be quite so eager for it if they knew that it qualified them to be first for the firing squad? Or would they see to it that the neon lights that spelled out their names were not quite so bright? It is little wonder that Jesus said to James and John, "You don't know what you are asking" (Mk 10:38).

Before he explained the other feature of true greatness, he brought in the remaining ten apostles (v. 42), for James and John weren't the only ones that day who needed this particular lesson. As so often happens, status-seeking proved irritating to the other disciples and put a strain on their fellowship.

Mark records, "When the ten heard it, they began to be indignant at James and John" (Mk 10:41 RSV). No doubt it stirred up their repressed love of prestige. How often we reveal our true character by what provokes our strongest reactions! The attitude being displayed by the disciples is characteristic of the Gentiles, those in the world outside God's covenant. But Jesus expects something quite different of his disciples—"Not so with you" (v. 43). So Jesus realized that all twelve of the apostles needed instruction and he, "Called them together and said, 'You know that those who are regarded as rulers of the Gentiles lord it over them, and their high officials exercise authority over them' " (Mk 10:42).

Jesus then gives them the second mark of true greatness which is the complete opposite of what is taken for granted in the world. It is the willingness to assume a humble role: "Whoever wants to become great among you must be your servant, and whoever want to be first must be slave of all. For even the Son of Man did not come to be served, but to serve, and to give his life as a ransom for many" (Mk 10:43-45).

Here, Jesus reveals how his conception of his mission was dominated by the servant of the Lord in Isaiah and that he expected his disciples to take it as a pattern for their own ministry. And, he practiced what he preached, supremely, of course, in his humiliating death, but also when he took the basin and towel and washed his disciples' feet. When Peter, after protests, submitted to it, Jesus added: "Now that I, your Lord and Teacher, have washed your feet, you should also wash one another's feet. I have set you an example, that you should do as I have done for you" (Jn 13:14-15).

This ought to affect the way we assess our ministry! In the light of Jesus' assessment of true greatness, who might we expect to have the front places in heaven? There will be ministers in tough inner-city situations, missionaries in remote stations, those with ability who, if given the opportunity of working in a nice suburb or a church in a strategic position, might have become world-famous. There is the little old lady, whose prayer life would put many an evangelical public performer to shame. There is the faithful soul who cleans the church and always has a gracious word for anyone who enters the building during the operation. Evangelists ought to appreciate that the contribution of those who provide them with their audience by inviting non-Christian neighbors is no less important than their own. It gives them little prestige, but their devotion is seen by God.

In other words, those who enjoy the prestige that their ministry gives them must not assume that the top places in heaven are reserved for bishops, well-known evangelists, occupants of prominent pulpits and convention speakers. Those who obey God's commandments and teach them to others "will be called great in the kingdom of heaven" (Mt 5:19). Indeed such obedience was valued by Jesus even more highly than physical relationship with him (Lk 8:21; 11:28). Those who are concerned about their status in the church ought to bear in mind one of the characteristic sayings of Jesus, "Many that are first will be last, and the last first."

Jesus ends his discussion with James and John with a reference to his approaching death. This expresses in clear terms both of the points he has been making. On the one hand, it shows that the leadership which he displayed depended on the extreme suffering of the cross. The writer to the Hebrews speaks of his death as an expression of leadership when he calls Jesus the "pioneer of our salvation." A pioneer is one who goes ahead of others, leading the way. That leading was made "perfect through suffering" (Heb 2:10). The death of Jesus is also the supreme demonstration that he came "not to be served but to serve." The pattern for this style of leadership is found in Isaiah's description of the humiliating death of the Servant of the Lord (ch 53). He was the "Servant King," as one of Graham Kendrick's songs describes him.

Many of us lay great emphasis on the death of Christ and the need for a truly biblical understanding of it. It lies at the center of our theology, and we regard it as an essential to the gospel we proclaim. How tragic it would be if we allowed our proclamation of such a gospel to become a pedestal for self-aggrandizement! Surely if the death of Christ means to us what we say it does, we should declare with Isaac Watts,

When I survey the wondrous cross,
On which the Prince of glory died,
My richest gain I count but loss,
and pour contempt on all my pride.[6]

## Questions for Individuals or Groups

1. Do you know any leaders who operate out of a love for power and prestige? Describe them.

2. What do you think causes some people to demand powerful roles in life? (pp. 130-31)

3. How can leaders protect themselves from becoming proud?

4. On page 132, the author gives James Packer's view of the meaning of success in ministry. Do you agree or disagree with this assessment? How would you define success in ministry?

5. Why do you think Jesus describes greatness in ministry as being costly? (pp. 133-34)

6. Why do you think Jesus describes a leader as being the "slave of all"? (p. 135)

7. How does Jesus' description of great leaders differ from what the world teaches? (pp. 135-36)

8. According to Jesus' definition, who are the "great" leaders in your church or fellowship group? (pp. 136-37)

9. How does Jesus' death on the cross affect the way in which you do ministry?

# 9

# OVERSENSITIVITY

## Timothy

TIMOTHY EMERGED AS A POTENTIAL LEADER WHEN HE WAS comparatively young, but this did not deter Paul from giving him responsibility. Most denominations have followed the same policy, ordaining young people as their ministers, without waiting for age to qualify them as "elders." Many who have made their mark have begun to do so in their early years. Charles Spurgeon, for example, having entered the pastorate at the age of seventeen, began his occupation of the pulpit at New Park Street (which was to make him famous) when he was only twenty. Business and industry today are now following the church in choosing young persons as their executives.

As with many gifted young people, who rise to prominence at an early age, Timothy was shy and sensitive. We have already met in Elijah's contemporary, Obadiah, one of similar disposition, and have seen how it provided him with sufficient imagination to cope with the delicate situation of living under Ahab's roof. It is, however, to Timothy that we must turn for the most detailed insight into the potential strengths and weaknesses of this kind of personality.

Paul leaves us in no doubt about the high regard he had for him. He was aware of his godly upbringing based on Old Testament Scripture (2 Tim 3:15), and of the influence of a mother and grandmother who were both believers (2 Tim 1:5). It seems, though, that his father was a pagan (Acts 16:1) which would explain why he had never been circumcised as a baby. Paul first met him when visiting Lystra, and called Timothy, "my son, whom I love, who is faithful in the Lord" (1 Cor 4:17; see also 1 Tim 1:2). Paul soon invited him to accompany him on his missionary travels (Acts 16:3). Timothy was his "fellow worker" (Rom 16:21), even to the extent of associating Timothy's name with his own when writing from Rome (Phil 1:1; Col 1:1; Philem 1). Paul's confidence in him can be measured by the way he entrusted him with important missions, such as the encouragement of persecuted Christians at Thessalonica (1 Thess 3:1-2). Indeed Paul goes as far as to say that there is no one whom he would sooner send as his delegate (Phil 2:19-23). Finally, by the time Paul, at the end of his life, wrote the letters to him which are preserved in the New Testament, Timothy has been left at Ephesus to supervise the work there, which included watching over the church's teaching, ordering its worship, appointing suitable leaders and other highly responsible tasks.

In the light of all that Paul entrusted to him it may come as a surprise to discover that he was a timid and sensitive young man, so much so that Paul felt it necessary to write to the church at Corinth about him: "If Timothy comes, see to it that he has nothing to fear while he is with you, for he is carrying on the work of the Lord, just as I am. No one, then, should refuse to accept him. Send him on his way in peace so that he may return to me. I am expecting him along with the brothers" (1 Cor 16:10-11). Timothy, then, must have been easily embarrassed, and needed to be put at ease. No doubt his youth added to his difficulties and invited people to adopt a patronizing attitude towards him. Did not Paul encourage him: "Don't let anyone look down on you because you are young" (1 Tim 4:12)?

In present day jargon we would describe him as an introvert; his interest tended to be directed toward himself and his own reactions, rather than outward to the external world. His over-concern about himself and what others thought of him made him nervous and fearful. It appears that Timothy did not enjoy good health and suffered from indigestion (1 Tim 5:23), a common accompaniment of a nervous disposition. (Was he suffering from a duodenal ulcer?) We are faced here with a well-defined personality, quite familiar today, even in some of the most distinguished Christian leaders.

## The Difficulties of a Sensitive Personality

There is no denying that sensitive and nervous people can be a baffling problem to those who have to work with them, and even to themselves. They may be touchy and awkward and, because of their concern with themselves and what others think of them, they are easily hurt if they are not receiving due recognition. Although they may do their best to suppress it, sensitive people are basically insecure and suspect that they are inadequate. So they will look for appreciation and reassurances of their success to overcome inner anxieties. They may find it difficult to receive criticism, be prone to misunderstand the comments of others and feel threatened. These tensions tend to be heightened in those whose occupation brings them before the public eye, and who depend for their success on the applause of others, such as entertainers and musicians and, of course, preachers!

Isolation is another situation which can reveal these same weaknesses and bring them to the surface. A notorious example has been the lonely mission station, where Christians have to learn to work amicably with associates they would never have chosen. It has not been unknown for missionary societies to bring a worker home because of interpersonal problems. As a further example, consider the frictions that can arise in a shared apartment amid the loneliness of a large city?

Another area of difficulty for sensitive Christians lies in the context of witness and evangelism. Natural shyness stands in the way of a clear confession of their Christian convictions before the world. When under pressure to conform to the lower moral standards of those around them, their temptation to compromise is very strong. After all, those who are anxious about what others think of them don't want to appear fanatical. A challenge to take part in some evangelistic activities can constitute a dilemma. On the one hand they desperately want to be well thought of by their fellow Christians by doing all that is expected of them, but the thought of approaching complete strangers in the street with the gospel, or doing the same thing on people's doorsteps, fills them with horror. How they envy their extroverted brothers and sisters who can do these things without turning a hair!

I recall a testimony meeting I attended in the days of my youth at which young Christians were challenged to stand up in public and "give their testimony." In between each response a verse of a hymn was sung which every time began with the words, "Ashamed to be a Christian." Those who failed to pluck up their courage and stand up and speak went away feeling very guilty. But if they were of the Timothy-type and unaccustomed to public speaking, they would have been nervous about standing on their feet before a meeting to speak about football, mathematics, their parents or any other topic.

So, what do we say about Christians whose sensitivity renders them easily offended, shy at meeting people and diffident about speaking to others about Christ? Does this disqualify them from Christian service and leadership? Or is there some way of overcoming these deficiencies? Before we look for the answer to this, there is another side of Timothy to be considered.

### The Potentiality of a Sensitive Personality
This comes out very clearly in Paul's assessment of Timothy in Philippians 2:19-24. To begin with he really cared for people to an extent which far surpassed Paul's other colleagues: "I have no one else like him, who takes a genuine interest in your welfare. For everyone looks out for his own interests, not those of Jesus Christ" (v. 20-21).

As we have seen, sensitive people can be dominated by a concern for themselves and what others think of them. But that need not be so. The word Paul uses here for "anxious" is the one in the Sermon on the Mount for caring for oneself—"about your life, what you will eat or drink; or about your body, what you will wear" (Mt 6:25). Timothy experienced such anxiety, but instead of it being for himself, it was for others and their needs. Sensitive persons are gifted with an imagination. They can put themselves in the shoes of others and understand how they feel. They are gentle in their dealings and avoid causing offense. They can get close to those they are seeking to help, like Ezekiel, who was called upon to minister to the exiles in Babylon and "sat among them for seven days—overwhelmed" (Ez 3:15). This is why a sensitive person has a great capacity for pastoral skills, and it seems that Paul detected this in Timothy.

Paul also found that he could work with him—a virtue which cannot be taken for granted in gifted Christian leaders! And here is a great advantage, because inability to get on harmoniously with others has often impaired the usefulness of capable Christian workers. Timothy could have allowed his sensitivity and feelings of insecurity to lead him to resent Paul for getting too much of the limelight and be irritated if his own contribution was not receiving due recognition. Yet there is no indication that Paul had any worries about Timothy on that score. Indeed, not only was he able to work with Paul, but he readily accepted working under him "as a son with a father" (Phil 2:22), willing to receive directions from him (vv. 19, 23). Learning to work under a senior person is a desirable part of the early training of a leader. Timothy passed that test well, being described by Guy King in the title of his exposition of 1 Timothy as "A leader led."

Here we have another application, similar to the one we made in the chapter about Moses, (p. 30) of the difference between living "according to the flesh" and "according to the Spirit" (Rom 8:4 RSV). Indwelling sin can exploit all our fleshly weaknesses, and sensitive persons are especially at risk here. Their sensitivity can render them likely to lose their temper, or experience jealousy and resentment.

The Holy Spirit, however, whose sanctifying work transforms character but not necessarily personality, can make great use of a sensitive disposition. It can come into its own in a situation which requires delicacy, where a thoughtless extrovert could do much damage. The potentiality for pastoral counselling is enormous when the natural gift of imagination is used to understand the difficulties of those in need. A sensitive person can be slow to cause offense and is more likely to be hurt than to cause hurt to others. So if we feel that this type of personality describes us, as it does many Christians, the answer is not to try to develop a thick skin under which to hide it, but to see that its potentialities are exploited by the Holy Spirit. While highly sensitive preachers may shrink from handling unpalatable doctrines of sin and judgment and may welcome respectable theological reasons for watering them down, they may take courage. The Holy Spirit can use their natural capacity to handle such topics with understanding and humility.

### Coping with Timidity

The difficulty that Christians like Timothy face is usually timidity, which makes it difficult to witness before the world and make an open stand for the truth—whether in the field of belief or moral standards. In Paul's second letter to Timothy we find that this is precisely the weakness that he detected in him as he called upon him: "Do not be ashamed to testify about our Lord" (1:8). Paul was in prison facing almost certain execution. How would Timothy continue when he no longer had Paul to lean upon? Would he have the courage to stand up to persecution? So he told him to "be strong in the grace that is in Christ Jesus" (2 Tim 2:1) and to "endure hardship with us like a good soldier of Jesus Christ" (2:3). Paul wondered whether Timothy would be embarrassed that a prominent Christian leader was being humiliated in a Roman prison. Paul instructed him not to be "ashamed of me his prisoner" (1:8). Out of a reluctance to gain the disapproval of others would he fail to stand out against some of the popular heresies which were afflicting the young churches? He is challenged: "guard the good deposit that was entrusted to you" (1:14).

Paul begins by reminding Timothy of the gifts which God has given him: "I remind you to fan into flame the gift of God, which is in you through the laying on of my hands. For God did not give us a spirit of timidity, but a spirit of power, of love and of self-discipline" (1:6-7). Exactly what "gift" Paul had in mind is difficult to say. He uses the Greek word *charisma* and makes an explicit reference to his ordination to Christian leadership. The same point was made in the first letter (4:14) and no doubt both writer and reader had a particular gift in mind. Whatever it was, here is a reassuring reminder that, no matter what demands are made upon us, and however inadequate we feel, God supplies the gift that is needed. It is a particular application of the promise, "And your strength will equal your days" (Deut 33:25). Although the Revised Standard Version renders Paul's main verb by "rekindle," the New International Version's "fan into a flame" is equally possible, so we need not assume that Timothy had lost his earlier enthusiasm which now needed to be recaptured. All that Paul is implying here is that any gift that God has given can atrophy through disuse. So we must "keep it alive, even ablaze, presumably by exercising the gift faithfully and by waiting upon God in prayer for its constant renewal."[1]

Paul then adds an encouragement to exercise all our God-given gifts. Whereas Timothy had been endowed with a particular gift, the statement which follows concerns what God has given to "us," that is to every Christian. And what God has given us is not a "spirit of timidity" or "cowardice." Now this is a most important general assertion, because the danger for persons who find themselves inhibited by fear is to resign themselves to it with the excuse, "I am made that way." Timothy may be shy and timid by nature, but that is no excuse for playing the coward.

During a battle in the nineteenth century, a young army recruit was trembling at his first taste of warfare. A bully of a sergeant noticed his plight and jeered at him. The young soldier admitted that he was frightened but added, "If you were half as frightened as I am, you would probably run away!" To acknowledge our natural fear is one thing, but to give way to cowardice is another. That would be to walk "according to the flesh" and not the Spirit.

So what has God given us? Paul sets out a threefold provision which God has made for all of us to counter our natural fears. The first is "the spirit of power." This is not a powerful personality which Timothy undoubtedly lacked, but rather the power which has enabled many a naturally timid Christian to develop a humble boldness in God's work. Martyn Lloyd-Jones has given a very useful description of what that power can mean:

> Here is a power even for weaklings . . . Are you afraid that you will not be able to live the Christian life? The answer is "Work out your own salvation with fear and trembling, for it is God that worketh in you both to will and to do." The fear and the trembling remain. That is partly your temperament, but you are able to work by the "power that worketh in you both to will and to do."[2]

This power can be proved in the most extreme circumstances, including the cruel persecution confronting the church when Paul was writing to Timothy. Subsequent church history can supply some moving examples. Martyn Lloyd-Jones continues:

> That is one of the most glorious things in the long history of the Church, and it is still happening. I never tire of telling Christians to read the stories of the martyrs and the Confes-

sors and the Protestant Fathers, of the Puritans and the Cove-
nanters. Read their stories and you will find not only strong,
courageous men, you will find weak women and girls and
even little children dying gloriously for Christ's sake. They
could not in and of themselves, but they were given the spirit
of power.

Together with power God gives love. Here is an essential com-
bination, because power without love can be dangerous and
unattractive, and there have been many ugly examples in the
world. Moreover, love is an antidote to fear (1 Jn 4:18). Learning to love helps to overcome the self-centeredness which can
be one of the weaknesses of a sensitive person. The more we
are taken up with God's love for us and, through us to others,
the less room there is for our fears, anxieties and over-concern
about what others think of us. I am impressed by the love
shown for their persecutors by many who have died for their
faith, and the way they have followed the example of Jesus who
prayed for those who were crucifying him.

This brings us to the third grace that God gives. Translators
have offered a number of alternatives to bring out what Paul was
saying: "self-control" (RSV), "self-discipline" (NIV), while J. B.
Phillips suggests "a sound mind" (KJV). What Paul seems to
have in mind is a life ordered by a balanced mind. There is no
need to appear eccentric or odd or to display the traits which
a sensitive Christian would want to avoid at all costs. In a useful
little book first published in 1908 with the title, *Christian Sanity*,
Dr. A. T. Schofield, tracing the use of the Greek word through
the rest of the New Testament, commented on Paul's use of it
here, "Spiritual power is often made an excuse for extravagan-
ces of conduct; not so here. Love, too, is made to condone all
sorts of excesses; not so here. With both power and love are
coupled, to maintain the balance of Christian conduct, the es-

sential element of a sane mind."[3]

Having reminded Timothy of these endowments which every Christian has received from God, and the special gift which Timothy had received for his particular ministry, Paul next proceeds to get to grips with Timothy's principal need which was to overcome his natural timidity. Timothy needed to learn not to be ashamed of the gospel, but to "testify about our Lord" (2 Tim 1:8). Timothy would have been only too aware that in a Greek city of those days the gospel of a crucified Savior would have been dismissed as ridiculous (1 Cor 1:23), and maybe Paul had told him of the jeers of the intelligentsia of Athens which had greeted his reference to the resurrection of Jesus (Acts 17:32). Timothy may well have felt a blush come to his cheeks when he attempted to speak on such matters. And this applies not only to those whom we normally regard as timid.

Lunn and Lean have taken note of the assessment of observers who "have attributed the declining influence of Christianity in recent years, in large measure to a failure of nerve on the part of Christians."[4] The forces of unbelief often seem overwhelming, having enlisted the support of many who are "mighty after the flesh" which, for Timothy, included Imperial Rome. For him there was the added embarrassment that Paul, the Gospel's leading advocate, was in prison, so there was the additional appeal by Paul not to be ashamed "of me his prisoner." Paul had good reason for making this point, as he had already been let down by many he regarded as his supporters (2 Tim 1:15; 4:16). The sight of other Christians being humiliated is no help to anyone like Timothy. Yet Paul's imprisonment is no defeat, for he described himself not as a prisoner of Rome, but as "his prisoner." Furthermore he encouraged Timothy not only to be unashamed but to be prepared to "join with me in suffering for the gospel by the power of God" (2 Tim 1:8).

The question which obviously presses upon us is how a shy Christian like Timothy is to become unashamed. We have already seen that it is not the method of the Holy Spirit to change temperament which, in the case of Timothy, would involve making him insensitive and rob him of an important element in his gifts as a pastor. Moses never lost his feeling of inadequacy, but instead it was used to engender the meekness for which he became renowned. How then was Paul to prepare Timothy for the battle? The answer is basically simple. It was to face Timothy again with the Gospel which had been committed to him.

Paul's approach at this point is to say nothing more about Timothy himself, not even about God's work in him, but to turn his attention away to the gospel which he had been called upon to guard, and to remind him of those aspects of it of which there was no need to be ashamed. And Paul certainly practiced what he was now preaching to Timothy. An example of this is the fine statement in his first chapter to the Romans which begins, "I am not ashamed of the gospel" (Rom 1:16). Note carefully his reasons for being unashamed. It is not his natural courage, nor some spiritual blessing which had transformed him from coward to hero. In fact he says nothing about himself at all. His reason for being unashamed is found simply in the gospel itself which, he declares "is the power of God for the salvation of everyone who believes."

Paul follows exactly the same line with Timothy. Having called on him to be unashamed and willing to suffer for the gospel (2 Tim 1:8), he asserts some of its great facts (vv. 9-10), because of which he himself is unashamed and willing to suffer (vv. 11-12). The Apostle's thinking is brought out by J. B. Phillips' paraphrase: "It is *this Gospel* that I am commissioned to proclaim; it is of *this Gospel* that I am appointed both Special

Messenger and Teacher, and it is for *this Gospel* that I am now suffering these things. Yet I am not in the least ashamed."[5] (italics mine).

Now, what does this gospel, which Paul takes such pride in, consist of? He selects a number of features which illustrate his main point, but the one which attracts our particular attention is that Christ has "destroyed death and has brought life and immortality to light through the gospel" (v. 10).

Paul could hardly have hit upon a more telling example of a gospel truth of which there was no need for shame. If there was anything to which first-century people were in bondage, it was the fear of death. Of this there is abundant evidence in both Latin and Greek writers. Their view of death is overshadowed by a feeling of hopelessness. Theocritus wrote, "There is hope for those who are alive, but those who have died are without hope." Aeschylus resigned himself to the view, "Once a man dies there is no resurrection." There are pathetic examples in letters of vain attempts to comfort the bereaved. Inscriptions on pagan tombs express the same despair such as, "I was not; I became; I am not; I care not." All this is in marked contrast to the joyful hope and confidence expressed on Christian tombs of the early centuries. And the reason for this is clear—the gospel of Christ is the perfect answer to the challenge of death. In that case why should any first-century Christian, even someone as timid as Timothy, be ashamed of it?

The situation is not much different in the last part of the twentieth century. Bereaved persons sometimes complain of how they are shunned by friends who pretend not to have seen them when passing in the street. This is not because of unfriendliness or lack of care, but because they find themselves at a loss for any meaningful response to the fact of death. Modern writers describe how death has become an unmentionable topic. This is how David Winter has portrayed it:

All sorts of conspiracies are indulged in to keep from the
dying person any knowledge of his true condition, and when
he does finally die enormous precautions are taken to ensure
that his passing upsets or disturbs as few people as possible,
A whole profession has built up around the euphemisms of
death and burial: casket (for coffin), chapel of rest (for mor-
tuary), the deceased (for the cadaver), floral tributes (for
wreaths), interment (for burial), and so on. The dead, who
were a source of comfort and inspiration to our forefathers—
are frankly an embarrassment to us. They remind us of our
own mortality, and we prefer to think ourselves immortal.[6]

A Christian has no need for this kind of escapism since Christ
has "abolished death." This does not mean that death no
longer exists, or that the thought of it ceases to be unpleasant.
Death is still described in the New Testament as an enemy, but
an enemy which has lost its terrors. "Nullified" would be a fair
translation of Paul's term in the resurrection chapter, 1 Corinthians 15. There, death is said to be like a venomous snake
which has lost its poison duct. Both death and snakes are unpleasant, especially for those who are squeamish about either,
but they are quite harmless. Moreover, death, distasteful though
the thought of it may be, is the gateway to the fuller life "with
Christ, which is better by far" (Phil 1:23). So the Christian is
glad to read about it in the Scriptures, sing about it in hymns
and witness to a gospel which brings victory over it.

This, however, is not the only aspect of the gospel which
takes away any excuse for being ashamed. Paul speaks of God
who has "saved us and called us to a holy life" (2 Tim 1:9).
Salvation and holiness mean more than forgiveness of our sins
so that we can face God after death, but have to do with the
quality the gospel imparts to this present earthly life and victory

over the spiritual foes which are out to ruin it.

Here is something of which the world knows nothing. Not even the most starry-eyed secular optimists can claim that this century has shown much promise of the golden age which was anticipated by their predecessors at its dawn. In spite of the vast amount of knowledge now at human disposal, there is little sign of the utopia that was once thought to be only just around the corner, nor of the "loftier race than e'er the world hath known" (John Addington Symonds). No Christian need be surprised at that because human problems are basically spiritual and moral and can be fully overcome only by the gospel. If modern people without Christ had succeeded in making a paradise out of this world, there might be some excuse for Christians to feel ashamed. But until that happens, why should Christians be embarrassed about what they believe?

I well remember a timid young Christian whose entire stance was transformed by bringing into play the issues we have been considering. It seems that his coworkers realized his weakness and took advantage of it as they frequently poked fun at his beliefs and moral standards, and made life quite miserable for him. One day he decided to remain passive no more and that attack was the best method of defense. So, taking what little courage he had in both hands, he addressed his colleagues with some fundamental questions—such as, what had they to say to the person who had ruined his marriage through sin, to someone seeking the meaning of life, to those afraid of death and so on. For once there was silence and even the most loud-mouthed had nothing to say. "So," he went on, "you are all experts at sneering at what I stand for, but when I challenge you to say something positive you have nothing to say." He had no more trouble from then on, and no one could have accused him again of being ashamed of being a Christian.

## The Need for Strong Convictions

Paul next shares with Timothy what lies at the heart of his own confidence and his shameless witness. Here is how he states his position: "I am not ashamed, because I know whom I have believed, and am convinced that he is able to guard what I have entrusted to him for that day" (2 Tim 1:12). Paul derived his confidence from his strong convictions. In a similar context where he writes of being afflicted, perplexed and persecuted, he gives the same reason for speaking out for Christ: "It is written: 'I believed; therefore I have spoken.' With that same spirit of faith we also believe and therefore speak, because we know that the one who raised the Lord Jesus from the dead will also raise us with Jesus and present us with you in his presence" (2 Cor 4:13-14).

"I believed and so I spoke" was the reason that the disciples refused to be silenced by the same Jerusalem authorities who had sent their Master to the cross. Christians who speak with conviction need to be sure of what they believe. In the tough days of the seventeenth century, the Puritan, Thomas Watson, whose convictions cost him a fair share of ill treatment, in the introductory chapter of his *Body of Divinity* made the observation: "Such as are not settled in the faith can never suffer for it. Sceptics in religion hardly ever prove martyrs."[7]

In order to see what lay behind Paul's position we need to look a little more closely at his wording. The tenses are important but are somewhat obscured in translation. Literally, it would be, "I know whom I have believed, and I have been persuaded." These perfect tenses refer to something completed in the past and now a present fact. What Paul is saying, then, amounts to this: in the past he has settled once and for all the truth of what he believes. This he has presumably done on objective grounds outside of himself, for nothing that has happened to him since has changed it. If he has already settled that the evidence points unmistakably to the conclusion that Jesus rose from the dead (as in fact he shows in 1 Corinthians 15), then his present difficulties make no difference. That is an issue he has looked into in the past and settled once and for all.

This conviction had a very relevant application to Timothy as a leader entrusted with preserving the gospel in its fullness and purity for future generations. This is a reason for following the Revised Standard Version rendering of the last part of 2 Timothy 1:12—"what has been entrusted to me." This is literally "my deposit," a word which is repeated in verse 14 where it is applied to Timothy. Some versions, including the King James take it as "what I have entrusted with God." This is grammatically quite possible and declares a familiar biblical truth. But it fits the present context to follow the Revised Standard Version and regard it as what God has committed to me—the gospel. It is of this responsibility that Paul reminds Timothy in verse 14, and Paul's own testimony in verse 12 provides an assurance that God can be trusted to enable Timothy to discharge that responsibility faithfully.

How is this timid young man to develop a boldness in standing for Christian truth when he no longer has Paul to lean on? First he must not give into his weakness under the assumption that cowardice is his God-given lot. At the same time he must not lose sight of the gifts God has given him. These include the particular gift which God has provided to enable Timothy to fulfill the particular ministry to which he has called him. This must not be allowed to waste away from disuse. Then there are the gifts of love, power and a sound mind which are available to every Christian. Above all, he needs a firm grip on the basic truths of the gospel, a confidence in their relevance and strong convictions about their truth. This is essential equipment for any Christian leader, not least a shy and sensitive one.

We are faced here with a lesson which all Christians, and not only sensitive, introverted leaders, need to learn—stress the objective rather than the subjective. Unfortunately, the treatment often offered to deal with tensions and anxieties is to feed them with subjective experiences which tend to make matters worse. If such a person suffers from mood swings, a mountaintop experience one week can cause the pendulum to swing just as far in the opposite direction the next. An undue emphasis and reliance on inner feelings can hinder growth toward spiritual maturity.

There have been some notable examples in history of those who have been hampered by excessive introspection. John Wesley seems to have come into this category, at least in his earlier years when he was taken up with the "inner witness" and looking inwardly at himself and his feelings for evidence of it. He was constantly trying to evaluate his own faith. Arnold Dallimore has described him: "Rather, as we have noticed, he had learned to emphasis faith as a subjective experience—and, as a result, his thought turned inward, there to recognize his weaknesses and to concern itself with what measure of faith he might possess."[8] Dallimore maintains that it was this tendency which hindered him from appreciating the doctrines of grace and robbed him of the very assurance he was seeking. Furthermore, as Dallimore also points out: "It will be recognized that while in this condition Wesley could not be a really effective preacher. Powerful preaching requires clear views and strong convictions, and though he could be dogmatic regarding 'salvation by faith,' there was little else of his newly acquired doctrinal position that he could declare with certainty."[9] In time Wesley learned a better way although, in the opinion of Dallimore, the uncertainties of those earlier years left their mark on the rest of his life and ministry.

One of the greatest needs of the sensitive introverted Christian then, is to keep constantly in view the objective facts about Christ. To do this is a way of strength for any Christian in times of weakness, because they do not depend for their truth on our changing feelings. So we need to master these truths and develop firm convictions about them. This can be a backbone to an otherwise spineless Christian.

## Questions for Individuals or Groups

1. Do you have any friends like Timothy who are sensitive? What are they like? (pp. 140-42)

2. What does Paul's model teach you about how to care for a sensitive person? (pp. 140-41)

3. Have you ever encountered the problem of sensitivity when it inhibits witnessing or evangelizing?

How have the author's comments on pages 142-43 helped you to understand the difficulties of public speaking for some Christians?

4. What are the potential benefits of a sensitive personality in a leader? (pp. 143-45)

5. The encouragement which Paul gave to Timothy (pp. 145-150) applies equally to all believers. How does it help you to know that you have a spirit of power, love and self-control as you continue in ministry?

6. How did Paul explain to Timothy that he should have no shame in declaring the gospel? (p. 150)

Why would this have had particular significance for Timothy? (p. 151)

7. In your own words, how does Paul describe the source of his convictions? (pp. 154-55)

8. How will Timothy be enabled to carry on without Paul? (pp. 155-56)

9. What does the author mean when he says "stress the objective rather than the subjective"? (p. 156)

How has it helped you in ministry when you have done this?

# 10

# CRITICISM

## Paul

ONE OF THE GREATEST TRIALS OF FULL-TIME CHRISTIAN MINISTRY
is criticism. Few, if any, escape it altogether, while some have
to undergo it in its cruelest form. When speaking on this subject
at ministers' meetings, I have been struck by the numbers who
have told me how they have had to suffer in this way, sometimes to the detriment of their health. Emotional persecution
can be especially difficult to bear. Those who have sensitive
consciences can readily be burdened with feelings of intense
guilt when they are blamed for anything that is wrong in a
church, or for failing to achieve the impossible ideals which are
set for them. Thus, dread is another emotion familiar to many
in leadership positions.

I was told by a friend, who was working for a society which
involved visiting Episcopalian clergy, how many confessed to

him their dread of the annual church meeting. Baptist ministers have described to me the nightmare of having to face a vote
of confidence at a church meeting brought about by deacons
plotting their removal. A minister, who had been counselling
colleagues in his own denomination, spoke of many who had
resigned from the Christian ministry through being unable to
cope with criticism and opposition. Many years ago, I remember being amazed to learn that a man who was a household name at Bible conventions had twice been forced out (or
"starved out") of his ministry positions.

All public figures are at risk in this respect. Their actions can
be discussed by folk who know only a fraction of the facts. A
person who wants to denigrate them can always find someone
who will listen to the prosecution and reach a verdict of guilty
without hearing any defense the slandered leader might offer,
and Christians are as adept at this kind of thing as anyone.
Innuendos, exaggerations, speculations as to their motives and
what amounts to criticizing someone for not being in two places
at once can all be used to tarnish reputations.

A minister who was victim of a gossip campaign of this kind
was accused by some of being too charismatic and by others of
not being charismatic enough. Some thought him too autocratic, while others felt his leadership was not strong enough. Unkind interpretations were put on his actions and some of the
things which he said. After a time, so I was told, there was not
a person of note in the church who did not want his resignation. Many would crack under such a strain but that man, no
doubt by the grace of God, continued for many years, and
during that time, his public image changed for the better. Some
of his detractors left the church, while others had second
thoughts about the unkind gossip which they had listened to.

Politics and religion are very similar in the behavior associated with them. I knew of a home where both topics were forbidden as subjects for discussion because of the heated arguments and breakdown in relationships they had produced. Politicians, who are probably polite and well-mannered at other times, will be abusive and arrogant with those who dare to hold different political opinions. Religion is the same. Arguing strongly held differing opinions can lead to all kinds of trouble. Eight- and nine-letter theological, swear words like Arminian and Calvinist fly. The correspondence columns in some church newspapers can be as full of arrogance as they are lacking in love, and I well remember hiding away one offending journal which used to come into our house, lest any non-Christian visitor might chance on some very unedifying reading. In a local church some will descend to all kinds of intrigue and even deceit out of determination to get their own way.

It is sad to have to admit that evangelicals are often the worst offenders, especially when they become intense about their opinions. I know of an evangelical who was pitied by those interviewing him for ordination because "evangelicals have a reputation for giving their ministers a bad time." Then there was the evangelical pastor who went to a church where there were few who shared his convictions. As he faithfully expounded Bible truth, people gradually responded. Evangelical believers joined from other churches, until eventually he had a completely evangelical church. "Then," he said, "my troubles began!" And lest we imagine that such behavior by evangelicals is only a modern phenomenon, church history has some ugly examples such as the eighteenth-century revival in Britain and America.

**New Testament Christians and Criticism**
The New Testament can also furnish examples of destructive

criticism, and a leader who had his share of it was none other than Paul. From the beginning of his ministry he learned to live with opposition. He suffered from opponents of the gospel outside the church, like the unbelievers who stoned him at Lystra and at Rome where his life ended, as he probably always suspected it would, by execution. At the same time he had to cope with heretics within the church, who tried to undermine his ministry, as did the Judaizers at Galatia, which accounts for the extreme distress he displays in his letter to the Galatians.

But what seemed to get under his skin more than anything else was criticism from those at Corinth who claimed to be spiritual. We read of him defending himself against failure to visit them (2 Cor 1:15-17)—that has a familiar ring for many of us! And he has to deal with questions raised about his handling of money (2 Cor 12:14-18).

Examples like this are trivial compared with the way they questioned his motives, his methods and his message, criticizing his character and even his appearance. Perhaps worst of all, they cast doubts on his authority as an apostle and his fitness for the office. There was, of course, nothing new in this. A case we have already considered was Moses. Not only did he have to contend with the Egyptians and later, the unfriendly tribes encountered during the wilderness wanderings, but the very people whom he was leading. Whenever anything went wrong, even when it was through their own sins and failings, Moses was on hand to receive the blame. And, human as he was, it sometimes got the better of him.

In coping with the criticism he received from Corinth, Paul was not fooled by their apparent spirituality. It is true that they were well endowed with spiritual gifts, as Paul acknowledged (1 Cor 1:7) but that did not mean that they were far advanced in practical sanctification. Indeed he told them plainly, "Brothers,

I could not address you as spiritual but as worldly—mere infants in Christ," and a symptom of their carnality and immaturity was their unintelligent attitude toward the comparative merits of church leaders (1 Cor 3:1-4).

Fleshly behavior among those who appear to be "spiritual" is the subject of a very perceptive chapter by Richard Lovelace entitled, "How revivals go wrong." He faces the unwelcome fact of history that an undoubted movement of the Spirit can be accompanied by the most appalling behavior on the part of those who claim to have been blessed. Lovelace explains it by a reminder of the solemn reality of indwelling sin which persists after conversion and the new birth, and makes itself felt even in times of revival. Here is how Lovelace accounts for it: "It might appear that the outpouring of the Spirit should quench the fire of sin, and this is certainly true in some measure. But there are times when that outpouring causes sin to flare up like a fire which has just been drenched in kerosene. Sin, rather than being quenched, is merely diverted into new channels." The result Lovelace describes as "ugly forms of spiritual flesh or fleshly spirituality."[1]

When people show signs of spirituality such as soundness in doctrine, attending prayer meetings and involvement in youth work, that does not necessarily indicate spiritual maturity. This is why we can encounter fleshly behavior where we least expect it. Even prayer meetings can be the center of intrigue and malicious gossip! A particularly insidious and common form of Lovelace's "spiritual flesh" is spiritual pride. I was once advised by a church member to accede to the wishes of "the more spiritual in the church," and it was noticeable that he used this expression interchangeably with the first personal pronoun! Laying claim to a superior spirituality is rarely a healthy exercise.

## Coping with Criticism

In 2 Corinthians 10 Paul shows how he copes with the criticism he is receiving from the Corinthians. Paul does reveal the specific accusations being directed at him, although we may feel as though we are listening to only one side of a telephone conversation. In verse 1 he quotes his critics by saying, "I, Paul, who am 'timid' when face to face with you, but 'bold' when away" (v. 1). He is being accused of being like those who don't have faith in their convictions when face to face with those with whom they disagree, but are outspoken when at a safe distance. Paul is more specific in verse 10: "For some say, 'His letters are weighty and forceful, but in person he is unimpressive and his speaking amounts to nothing.'"

Modern examples could perhaps be found among those who write angry, controversial letters to the Christian press, but who are not nearly so formidable when you meet them. It is clear from Paul's remarks in the following verses that he is not prepared to admit to such an inconsistency. The other charge he outlines in verse 2 where he refers to those who "think of us as if we walked according to the flesh" (KJV). They, it seems, were disputing the spiritual quality of his ministry.

Our purpose is not to go into all the details of how Paul answered these and other criticisms, but to discover his attitude to himself and how he presented himself to his critics. This is always an important question when others are taking a low view of us and our work. How do we regard ourselves? Do we humbly agree with our detractors and allow them to walk all over us, or do we defend ourselves and try to prove our worth?

It is very clear how Paul would have answered such a question. His attitude toward himself was twofold. He had a high view of his office, but kept to a low view of himself, the holder of that office. It meant that he saw his position in the church as a privilege of which he was unworthy but was his by God's grace alone: "Although I am less than the least of all God's people, this grace was given to me: to preach to the Gentiles the unsearchable riches of Christ" (Eph 3:8). He maintained this attitude not least when he was faced with the criticism heaped on him by the Corinthians. Unfortunately, there are those today who do just the opposite and downgrade their office, while holding an inordinately high view of themselves.

## Paul's View of His Office

Paul begins by asserting his apostolic authority with the emphatic "I, Paul" (2 Cor 10:1). Although it is, according to P. E. Hughes, "implicit rather than overtly stated,"[2] we can be reasonably sure that this was a reminder of his apostolic office and that his first readers would have understood it as such. They had already read the assertion of his apostleship in the opening sentence of the epistle, "Paul, called to be an apostle of Christ Jesus by the will of God," which was the way he began all of his epistles. And if they think he has overdone his assertions of authority, they ought not to feel in any way threatened because it is for the good of the church: "You may think that I have boasted unduly of my authority (which the Lord gave me, remember, to build you up not to break you down), but I don't think I have done anything to be ashamed of" (v. 8 J. B. Phillips).

No matter how his detractors may have tried to belittle his authority, Paul was in no doubt that he was as much an apostle as Peter, John or anyone else. "Am I not an apostle? Have I not seen Jesus our Lord?" he asked (1 Cor 9:1). In chapter 15 he shows that by this he meant that he, along with many others, was a qualified witness of the resurrection (v. 8), the main criterion recognized in Acts 1 when a replacement was being sought for Judas Iscariot[3] (see also Acts 10:41; 13:31). He added further support to his apostolic claims when confronting the heretics at Galatia (Gal 1:11—2:10). Note that this also included a recognition by the Jerusalem leaders—James, Peter and John—who were called to the Jews, while Paul had been called to work with the Gentiles. (Gal 2:7-9)

While Paul was taking this high view of the position that God had given him, he did not lose the humble view of himself. As soon as he had referred to the appearance of the risen Christ to him (which established his apostolic authority), he described himself: "I am the least of the apostles and do not even deserve to be called an apostle, because I persecuted the church of God. But by the grace of God I am what I am" (1 Cor 15:9-10). Even though he claimed to work harder in that office than others, he said it was "not I, but the grace of God that was with me" (v. 10). Many years later, as his life was drawing to a close he was still describing himself as "the worst of sinners" (1 Tim 1:16).

Now none of us possesses an authority on a par with Paul, whose inspired writings form a large part of New Testament Scripture. Nor can we expect our flock to bow before our utterances in the way that first-century churches like the one at Corinth ought to have done before Paul's writings when they first received them. On the other hand we should be in no less doubt that the leadership we do exercise has been given to us by the Lord, and that the sphere where we exercise it is just as much "by the will of God" as was Paul's apostleship. Uncertainty regarding this will only weaken our resolve to withstand opposition. If we are in the place and position of God's choice, our members are free to disagree with us, because we are not infallible, but to rebel against us as God-appointed ministers is an offense. So Paul's prescription for unity in a church is: "To respect those who work hard among you, who are over you in the Lord and who admonish you. Hold them in the highest regard in love because of their work. Live in peace with each other" (1 Thess 5:12-13).

For God-given authority to be credible, however, leaders must recognize that they are also under authority, the authority of our Lord himself. It is to him that leaders are primarily accountable—not to their church members. The centurion detected this principle underlying our Lord's authority over disease and saw it mirrored in his own position as a military commander. Because he was under the authority of Rome, he could speak with that same authority (Lk 7:8). He was correct in seeing that the ground of Jesus' authority was similar, based on the Father's will (Jn 5:30; 6:38) to which Jesus was unreservedly committed.

Admittedly, it may be difficult to apply this principle in denominations where the pastor is appointed by a majority vote of the members and can be fired in the same way. (I have served under the Anglican system, which is rather different, and am in no position to give advice.) Nevertheless, most of us are paid by the churches we serve, and there is a danger of allowing that fact to dictate our behavior, although such an approach has no scriptural support. Paul says that "elders who direct the affairs of the church well are worthy of double honor, especially those whose work is preaching and teaching" (1 Tim 5:17), but they are still expected to "direct."

Early in 1 Corinthians, having described himself and his apostolic peers as "servants of Christ and as those entrusted with secret things of God" (1 Cor 4:1), Paul gives his critics a salutary reminder that he will one day have to render an account of his ministry to the Lord and not to them (1 Cor 4:3-5). Some church members today need to be reminded of that.

And so, for that matter, do leaders who are over-concerned about what people think of them. This does not mean that Paul intends that we should ignore completely how others view us. He advises his young colleague that the leader "must also have a good reputation with outsiders, so he will not fall into disgrace and into the devil's trap" (1 Tim 3:7). Also Paul's aim for ministry is to "commend ourselves to every man's conscience" (2 Cor 4:2). He adds, however, "in the sight of God," because "there is a higher scrutiny than that of the human conscience,"[4] and what others say is not our final arbiter. The judgment of others is "a very small thing." Oh that those of us who are oppressed by what others say or who are always looking for human compliments could cut both their criticisms and adulations down to such a size!

That, however, is not the only judgment which Paul discounts, because he adds, "I do not even judge myself. I am not aware of anything against myself, but I am not thereby acquitted." We must not imagine that the judgment of others is corrected by the way he assesses himself, as he see dangers no less from that direction. "I am not aware of anything against myself," he writes because, like most of us, he gives himself the benefit of the doubt. We cannot be judge and jury in our own case. This is what Paul's opponents do and he refuses to compete with them and be like "those who write their own testimonials" (2 Cor 10:12, J. B. Phillips). Instead, he concludes, quoting the prophet Jeremiah: " 'Let him who boasts boast in the Lord.' For it is not the one who commends himself who is approved, but the one whom the Lord commends" (2 Cor 10:17-18).

What matters for Paul, then, is the judgment of God. This has particular advantages. For one thing it will be timely: "therefore do not pronounce judgment before the time, before the Lord comes." All the facts will be known because the Lord "will bring to light the things now hidden in darkness." The reason our judgments of one another are usually inadequate is that they are based on incomplete knowledge. Unlike many of those who listen to gossip, a court must hear the defense as well as the prosecution before reaching a verdict, the reliability of witnesses must be established (church members with undisciplined tongues need this test), and there may also be mitigating circumstances to take into account.

When the Lord comes, all the evidence will be before him. And what of the result? It is not what we usually expect of God's judgment: for one who can write "since then we know what it is to fear the Lord, we try to persuade men" (2 Cor 5:11) also looks forward to when "every man will receive his commendation from God." God's judgment of our ministry will be much fairer and kinder than that of many of our human critics. Christian leaders who are being given a hard time, if they are sincerely seeking to do God's will, may well look forward to that day.

How does Paul exercise that office of which he takes such a high view? Does it make him into a spiritual tyrant? The answer to this question follows from Paul's express desire to speak from "the meekness and gentleness of Christ" (2 Cor 10:1). No one could accuse him of "lording it over those entrusted to" him (1 Pet 5:3).

Paul uses three words to describe his style. The first is one of his favorites *parakaleo,* translated here (2 Cor 10:1) and elsewhere "beseech" (KJV), "entreat" (RSV), "appeal to" (NIV & NEB) or "encourage." The cognate noun *parakletos* is used of the Holy Spirit in John 14-16 and translated "Comforter" in the older translation and "Counselor" in many modern versions. Next he refers to his "meekness," meaning that he was not self-assertive or easily offended. George Duncan defines this as "the capacity to accept injury without resentment and praise without pride."[5] Additionally, there is "gentleness," described by the Greeks as "that quality which must enter in when justice, just because of its generality, is in danger of becoming unjust."[6] Both these qualities are "of Christ," the one who claimed to be "meek" (KJV) or "gentle" (NIV) "in heart" (Mt 11:29). When dealing with difficult church situations, we may have the intellectual ability to win arguments over less academic members of our congregation, but it does not necessarily bring healing. As George Duncan puts it, "there are two ways of opening a stiff lock: the one is to break it and the other is to oil it."[7] Paul steps down from his position of authority as he relates to people, including his critics, with sensitivity and understanding.

He wants to maintain this gentle style of ministry because if it does not work, he has only one alternative. So he writes, "begging you to make it unnecessary for me to be outspoken and stern in your presence" (2 Cor 10:2 J. B. Phillips). He leaves his readers in no doubt that if he needs to be stern he can be, as he warns them: "Let them realise that we can be just as 'impressive and moving' in person as they say we are in our letters" (v. 11 J. B. Phillips). The minister of a large congregation once confided to me, "I don't want to have to be autocratic," but it seemed that the behavior of some of his congregation would leave him with no other course. And any God-appointed leader must be prepared for that.

### Paul's View of Himself

Of himself, the holder of that office, Paul has a different view. At this point we must look again at the other criticism being levelled against him. He refers to "some which think of us as if we walked according to the flesh" (2 Cor 10:2 KJV). I choose the older version because it translates the Greek word *sarx* as "flesh," which is its true meaning. I have never been able to understand why the Revised Standard Version and the New International Version here and in other places, translate it as "world," which expresses a different, but related idea. "Flesh" refers to our own human weakness and not to the world around us. The New English Bible reads "moral weakness," while J. B. Phillips does justice to what Paul is saying with "those who persist in reckoning that our activities are on the purely human level." This could cover a wide variety of charges—such as, his style is only good psychology; he just likes the kudos; he's in it for the money.

Paul answers this charge by first admitting his humanity. Here is how various translators render the beginning of 2 Corinthians 10:3:

"Though we walk in the flesh . . ." *(en sarki,* KJV)

"Weak men we may be . . ." (NEB)

"The truth is that, although of course we lead normal human lives . . ." (Phillips)

He makes the same point earlier in this letter: "We have this treasure in jars of clay" (2 Cor 4:7).

Now if we are to benefit from Paul's example, it is essential not to gloss over this admission which he slips in. He does not wish to pretend that he is anything other than an ordinary human being with fleshly weaknesses just like anyone else. He is not an apostolic superman. By making the same acknowledgement, we can avoid many tensions and conflicts.

I remember many years ago being helped in this respect by a young contemporary. "You gave a great word" I commented on a sermon he had just preached. He could have given the pious and almost predictable reply, "Ah, Brother, it was the Lord who enabled me," and he would have meant it. Instead, giving me a nudge, and with a twinkle in his eye, he said, "I hoped you would say that!" He was human enough to appreciate a bit of praise and did not mind admitting it. This is emotionally healthy, and many intensely serious evangelicals would do well to emulate it.

I have heard it said that Christian ministry is the most guilt-ridden of all professions. For example some of us must give the impression of constant busyness because if we are caught relaxing, we immediately feel guilty—they might think we work only on Sundays! Some Victorian Christian biographers seem to have been under this kind of constraint when they were afraid to admit to any weaknesses in their spiritual heroes. I remember this being pointed out to me by a respectable churchwoman who did not share my evangelical background. I lent her an evangelical biography which I thought might impress her. She eventually returned it to me with the comment, "It's too good to be true" and I had to confess that she was right!

Paul's difficulties were intensified because many of his critics were, or thought they were, high-powered. Some boasted of a superior knowledge which Paul countered with the warning that "knowledge puffs up" (1 Cor 8:1). This is also a factor to be reckoned with today. An African leader once shared with me the problems of pastors who were undergoing severe pressures from their congregations who were better educated than they and found it difficult to accept their leadership.

A much-traveled preacher observed to me that severe problems are caused in some churches by those who are prima donnas in their own sphere and assume that they are far better qualified to run their church than the full-time minister, in spite of the pastor's training and experience. Professional people, academics and those in leading positions in business are among the chief culprits. "My husband is so accustomed to being the boss from Monday to Friday that he cannot forget it on Sunday" was how I once heard it explained. A mystified church member, who tried in vain to discover the issues behind the sad divisions in his church concluded, "It seems to be simply a matter of authority and who is to run the church." Then there was the businessman who reported to me on the troubles a pastor was having in a church he had visited in a developing country: "The trouble is that many of his members are professional missionaries who are convinced that they know best how the church should be led." I have heard the same said of retired clergy in a congregation.

How do leaders conduct themselves in such situations? Do we draw attention to the gifts and attainments which qualify us for our position? When a minister was going through a difficult time at a church meeting, a member took the opportunity, with no concern for the minister's feelings, to tell him in front of everyone else that he was not up to the job. How should he respond to such a humiliation?

Paul has left a clear example to follow in 2 Corinthians 11 where he admits his weaknesses, glorying in them as the setting in which to prove God's grace. In his case he had much going for him in which he could "boast" (a much used word in that chapter), such as his background and many costly and painful adventures, which could surpass anything his rivals could claim. But he lists them in order to show how stupid it all sounds when someone blows his own trumpet: "I am speaking as a fool" (v. 21); "I am out of my mind to talk like this" (v. 23). He discounts it all as he concludes, "If I must boast, I will boast of the things that show my weakness" (v. 30). In the following chapter he illustrates this better way as he recalls how God had three times refused his request to remove a "thorn in the flesh," whatever that may have been, and instead answered his prayer with the promise of special grace to endure it. The response, therefore, to those who criticize and humiliate us is not to try and improve our image. If Paul had done that, he would have been in danger of adding to the personality cult which was afflicting the Corinthian church by building up the "I am of Paul" party. Nor do we try to compete with the assumed expertise of our critics. Instead we admit our weakness and frailty and point to the all-sufficient grace of God.

### Paul's Style of Ministry
Although Paul acknowledges his human weakness, he does not pander to it. "We do not wage war after the flesh" (2 Cor 10:3 KJV). It is one thing to admit that you enjoy the praise of others; it is another to make their admiration the aim of your work. We may be honest enough to own up to a concern about money, but we need not allow it to become the main criterion when choosing an appointment, nor will we rely on financial induce-ments to attract workers.

Additionally, we must avoid the temptation to counter den-igration by trying to build up our own images. We do this by dragging in illustrations when speaking which reveal earlier successes, draw attention to our extensive travels or include a little name dropping. Many years ago I knew of a preacher who used all these devices. It did nothing to improve his image because, unknown to the silly man, he was a laughingstock in his church. Commercial advertising has no scruples about ap-pealing to the flesh when it exploits sexual weaknesses, the desire for self-display and selfish pleasure, but such methods are quite unacceptable in Christian work.

Another temptation we must resist is using the pulpit to pre-sent our side of a personal feud. I have known of preachers who have done that, albeit by careful innuendo, but the flesh-liness of it usually irritates the hearers and simply produces further discord. These are just some of the ways which will be spurned by those who refuse to "war after the flesh."

Paul has far more effective weapons to wield which "are not carnal, but mighty through God to the pulling down of strong-holds" (v. 4 KJV). Coping with ills within the church is part of the spiritual conflict in which we are engaged and, for such, carnal weapons are useless. "Carnal weapons such as human cleverness or ingenuity, organizing ability, eloquent diatribe, powerful propaganda, or reliance on charm or forcefulness of personality, are all in themselves quite unavailing in the cease-less task of pulling down the strongholds in which evil is en-trenched."[8] Attacking spiritual enemies with such weapons has been likened to attacking a modern tank with a can-opener. For pulling down the strongholds of the enemy, only spiritual weap-ons will suffice.

What are these spiritual weapons and the strongholds they are used to assault? One answer would be found in a cross reference to the list in Ephesians 6. But to continue with Paul's line of thought in 2 Corinthians 10:5, "We demolish arguments and every pretension that sets itself up against the knowledge of God, and we take captive every thought to make it obedient to Christ."

There are two particular points to notice. The first is that in place of the fleshly methods he has renounced, Paul appeals to the mind. This is apparent from his vocabulary—"argu-ments," "knowledge" and "every thought." The tension be-tween flesh and mind is something we all have to face as Paul confessed, "I myself in my mind am a slave to God's law, but in the sinful nature a slave to the law of sin" (Rom 7:25).

This is why Christians who live on their feelings are in special danger and why movements which exploit them tend to have their full share of moral problems and scandals. Reliance on feelings is notorious for leading Christians into error, when they settle questions of doctrine by what feels to be true, and matters of conduct by what feels right. This emphasis on the mind, frequently made in the New Testament, is especially significant in the present context, because criticism of others arises, as often as not, from irrational feelings. Rarely are they completely objective, but originate in prejudices, jealousies and so on.

This was brought home to me as a child when I overheard two adults criticizing the pastor of their church. "He said it with that sickly grin on his face" was the comment I clearly recall. But I had also heard that same smile described by others as "delightful" and "kindly," revealing what a godly man he was. Some of our judgments of others are shaped by the phenomenon which psychologists have called "projection"—by which we readily detect faults in others of which we are ourselves guilty. For example when the secretary of an organization was arranging publicity for a meeting, the speaker was very concerned that all his academic degrees should be indicated. She told me how surprised she was when she heard that this speaker had been to see the minister of his church to tell him he was too taken up with his status! In my early days in the ministry I once had a sleepless night because someone told me that large numbers of people in the church were saying things against me. I discovered later that the informant had herself been the one to encourage it, probably because I had followed the advice of someone whom she had been jealous of for many years.

It is examples like these that make one realize that critics often reveal more about themselves than the person they are

defaming. It is little wonder that Jesus said what he did about
removing the log of wood from our own eye before we presume
to deal with the speck of dust in someone else's (Mt 7:1-5). If
we are faced with critics who base their judgment of us on
fleshly, subjective feelings, how essential it is that our own
methods shall rise above theirs as we challenge them to use
their minds!

Our second observation concerns Paul's aim which, he says,
is to "take captive every thought to make it obedient to Christ."
Chapter 11 reveals what lay behind these instructions; they had
been listening to false apostles. Instead of their thinking being
"captive to obey Christ," they were in danger of being "led
astray from your sincere and pure devotion to Christ" (v. 3)
through being presented with "a Jesus other than the Jesus we
preached," "a different spirit" or "a different gospel" (v. 4).

This also has a contemporary ring about it because, as with
the Corinthians who were surrounded by pagan philosophy, it
is just as easy in the twentieth-century to imbibe the thinking
of the world, as we are bombarded with it through what we read
in our newspapers, hear on the radio and see on our television
screens. Well-educated people have the added danger of swal-
lowing some of the non-Christian presuppositions of the disciplines in which they have been trained, such as philosophy,
psychology, sociology, history, materialistic science and—it
must not be forgotten—liberal theology! Nor are those with
evangelical reputations exempt. But why should superspiritual,
highly gifted Christians like the Corinthians need such a warning about heretical teaching? The reason is that those who are
led by their fleshly feelings in criticizing a leader are just as
likely to go wrong doctrinally if they simply believe what feels
right is true.

"A sincere and pure devotion to Christ" is the key to every-

thing in the Christian life including unity in a church fellowship. It should be the means of bridging many barriers—racial,
tribal, social and surely, differences within a local church. Yet,
such an attitude towards Christ is the priority which many who
indulge in criticism seem to lack.

For instance a minister who was undergoing severe trials in
his church was asked how he managed to maintain his pulpit
ministry when under such pressure. He replied that he just
sought to uplift Christ as he had always done. It was surely a
tragedy that some were too concerned about their controversies
for a Christ-centered unity with their minister to mean much
to them.

For Paul obedience to Christ should be the end of all strife.
There was one particular occasion when he was the one to feel
the temptation to be critical of other preachers, and it seems
that there was some justification for it. But he laid his criticism
to one side with the assertion, "The important thing is that in
every way, whether from false motives or true, Christ is
preached. And because of this I rejoice" (Phil 1:18).

What then, according to Paul, is the way to respond to criticism? We shall, of course, be ready to ask ourselves if there is
any justification for it and if we have wronged anyone we shall,
like any other Christian, seek their forgiveness. But we must
never forget that it is to God that we are ultimately responsible.
Nor must we allow ourselves to undervalue the office God has
given us. This will be coupled with a humble view of ourselves
which attributes our position, gifts and successes to God's grace.
We shall continue to exercise our ministry with gentleness, yet
showing firmness where necessary. While admitting that we are
no more immune from fleshly weaknesses than our critics, we
shall never give in to them in ourselves, nor will we exploit
them in our detractors. Instead our aim will be to storm the

strongholds of people's minds with God's truth. Above all, our supreme objective will be, not to improve our image, nor to expect everyone to agree with us on every issue, but to uplift Christ and look for those who will find in this a unity with us.

## Questions for Individuals or Groups

1. When have you seen criticism greatly affect someone's ministry? What was the result?

2. Why do you think Christians get involved in the kind of bickering described here? (pp. 159-63)

3. Why is the leader's self-perception important to coping with criticism? (pp. 164-65)

4. How do you regard your authority as a leader?

5. Why is it important that we remain under the judgment of God and not those whom we minister to? (pp. 166-69)

6. Summarize Paul's philosophy of leadership? (pp. 170-74)

7. Have you known leaders who, like Paul, were willing to admit their faults? (pp. 171-74)

What were they like?

8. Why is it important for leaders to acknowledge their human side when dealing with criticism? (pp. 174-75)

9. How have you dealt with the temptation to build yourself up as you are involved in ministry? (p. 175)

10. Why does the author say "Christians who live on their feelings are in special danger"? (p. 176)

11. Why do you think Paul refused to criticize other pastors? (p. 178)

12. Summarize what you have learned about dealing with criticism based on Paul's model.

## Epilogue

My hope in writing this book in that it will encourage those who have the responsibility of Christian leadership and ministry to turn more often to Scripture for help with difficulties. We may be adept at teaching others but, as Paul wrote to Timothy along with much advice about his leadership of the churches, "Watch your life and doctrine closely" (1 Tim 4:16). We need to pay heed to the plain warnings regarding sexual temptations. "Flee the evil desires of youth" (2 Tim 2:22) is the terse way that Paul puts it to a young minister. Regarding the desire for prestige Jeremiah speaks just as abruptly: "Should you then seek great things for yourself? Seek them not" (Jer 45:5).

We can overcome or grow out of some of our weaknesses as Joseph and Elisha did. Many of our weaknesses, however, remain with us, as did Paul's "thorn in the flesh." But this does not mean a hopeless resignation, because God means them to be aids to our spiritual growth and the way we experience his power. The hall of fame in Hebrews 11 does not consist of those who were naturally strong, but those "whose weakness was turned to strength" (Heb 11:34). This, too, was the testimony of the apostle, as it should be Christian leaders who acknowledge their weakness and rely upon God's enabling grace:

> He said to me, "My grace is sufficient for you, for my power is made perfect in weakness." I will all the more gladly boast of my weaknesses, that the power of Christ may rest upon me . . . for when I am weak, then I am strong.
>
> (2 Cor 12:9-10)

# Notes

**Chapter One: Immaturity—Joseph**

[1]Dods, *Expositor's Bible* (London: Hodder and Stoughton, 1903), p. 322.
[2]Hercus, *Pages from God's Case Book* (Leicester, England: Inter-Varsity Fellowship, 1962), p. 116.
[3]Alexander Whyte, *Bible Characters*, 1 (London: Oliphants, 1952), p. 117.
[4]Ibid., p. 335.

**Chapter Two: Inadequacy—Moses**

[1]Cardinal Heenan, *The Times*, (London), February 19, 1969.
[2]Whyte, *Bible Characters*, p. 141.
[3]Quoted by H. Guntrip in *Psychology for Ministers and Social Workers* (London: Independent Press, 1949), p. 260.

**Chapter Three: Sexual Temptation—Sampson, David, Solomon**

[1]Sanders, *Men from God's School* (London: Marshall, Morgan and Scott, 1965), p.102.
[2]Cundall, *Judges* (London: Tyndale Press, 1968), p. 178.

**Chapter Four: Depression—Elijah**

[1]J. B. Phillips, *Your God is too Small* (London: Wyvern Books, 1952), p. 93.
[2]Whyte, *Bible Characters*, p. 363.
[3]Pink, *The Life of Elijah* (London: Banner of Truth Trust, 1956), p. 100.
[4]Mobbs, *Our Rebel Emotions* (London: Hodder and Stoughton, 1970), p. 28.

[5]Leavitt, *Managerial Psychology* (Chicago: University of Chicago Press, 1958), p. 50.

[6]As quoted in Dave Hunt and T. A. McMahon, *The Seduction of Christianity* (Eugene, Oregon: Harvest House, 1985), p. 200.

[7]Derek Kidner, *Psalms* (Downers Grove, Ill.: InterVarsity Press, 1975), p. 278.

[8]Paul Tournier, *Guilt and Grace* (London: Hodder and Stoughton, 1962), p. 153.

[9]Martyn Lloyd-Jones, *Spiritual Depression* (London: Pickering and Inglis, 1965), p. 165.

[10]Ibid., p. 172.

**Chapter Five: In the Shadow of a Mentor—Elisha**

[1]Whyte, *Bible Characters*, p. 368.

[2]Randolph S. Churchill, *Winston S. Churchill*, 1 (London: Heineman, 1966), p. 283.

[3]Ibid., p. 285.

[4]Whyte, *Bible Characters*, p. 370.

**Chapter Six: Marital Stress—Hosea**

[1]Derek Kidner, *The Message of Hosea: Love to the Loveless* (Downers Grove, Ill.: InterVarsity Press, 1981), p. 47.

[2]Ibid., p. 48.

[3]Ibid., p. 31.

**Chapter Seven: Impulsiveness—Peter**

[1]F. F. Bruce, *The Training of the Twelve* (Edinburgh: T. & T. Clark, 1911), p. 512.

[2]Temple, *Readings in St. John's Gospel* (London: MacMillan, 1949), p. 29.

[3]Stibbs, *Obeying God's Word* (London: Inter-Varsity Fellowship, 1967), p. 38.

[4]Ryle, *Five Christian Leaders of the Eighteenth Century* (London: Banner of Truth, 1960), p. 147.

[5]Morris, *The Gospel According to John* (London: Marshall, Morgan & Scott, 1972), p. 390.

[6]Ibid., p. 509f.

[7]Cranfield: *The First Epistle of Peter* (London: SCM Press, 1950), p. 108.

[8]Ibid., p. 112.

**Chapter Eight: The Love of Power and Prestige—James and John**

[1]Guntrip, *Psychology for Ministers*, p. 70.

[2]Richard Lovelace, *Dynamics of Spiritual Life* (Downers Grove, Ill.: InterVarsity

Press, 1981), p. 248.

[3]James Packer, *Christianity Today*, August 1988, p. 15.

[4]Peter Drucker, *Drucker on Management* (Management Publications Ltd, 1964), p. 15.

[5]R. A. Cole, *St. Mark* (London: Tyndale Press, 1961), p. 169.

[6]Isaac Watts, "When I Survey the Wondrous Cross."

**Chapter Nine: Oversensitivity—Timothy**

[1]John R. W. Stott, *The Message of 2 Timothy: Guard the Gospel* (Downers Grove, Ill.: InterVarsity Press, 1973), p. 30.

[2]D. Martyn Lloyd-Jones, *Spiritual Depression* (London: Pickering and Inglis, 1965), p. 101.

[3]A. T. Schofield, *Christian Sanity* (London: Oliphants, 1965), p. 25.

[4]Arnold Lunn and Garth Lean, *Christian Counter-Attack* (London: Blandford Press, 1969), p. 1.

[5]J. B. Phillips, *Letters to Young Churches* (London: Geoffrey Bless, 1947), p. 148.

[6]David Winter, *Hereafter* (London: Hodder and Stoughton, 1972), p. 13.

[7]Thomas Watson, *A Body of Divinity* (London: Banner of Truth Trust, 1958), p. 2.

[8]Arnold Dallimore, *George Whitefield*, 1 (Banner of Truth Trust, 1970), p.193.

[9]Ibid., p. 197.

**Chapter Ten: Criticism—Paul**

[1]Lovelace, *Dynamics of Spiritual Life*, p. 244.

[2]P. E. Hughes, *Paul's Second Epistle to the Corinthians* (London: Marshall, Morgan and Scott, 1962), p. 344.

[3]It is the view of some that Paul was in fact God's choice to restore their number to twelve and that the eleven were acting without any direction from the Lord, except in the qualifications they had enumerated.

[4]Hughes, *Paul's Second Epistle*, p. 124.

[5]George B. Duncan, *Pastor and People* (Waco, Tex.: Word Books, 1972) p. 97.

[6]William Barclay, *The Letters to the Corinthians* (St. Andrew Press, 1954) p. 266.

[7]George B. Duncan, *Pastor and People*, p. 97.

[8]R. V. G. Tasker, *The Second Epistle of Paul to the Corinthians* (London: Tyndale Press, 1958) p. 134.